REVIVING THE CHURCH | REACHING THE LOST

JEHOVAH JIREH *ministries*

THE LORD WHO PROVIDES

Jehovah Jireh Ministries was founded in 2019 by Dr. Ralph and Tammy Jenkins with the mission to bring the gospel to people groups around the world. We focus on planting churches, training pastors, and holding revivals and crusades wherever God leads us. Currently, much of our work is concentrated in India and Pakistan, where we have witnessed over 25,000 people come to Christ since the ministry began.

Jehovah Jireh Ministries operates prayer and conference centers in both India and Pakistan, where we equip national pastors to preach the gospel and shepherd their congregations. Lord willing, we plan to establish Jehovah Jireh Ministry Bible Colleges in both countries by 2025.

We also run a Children's Home in India, where we provide for the children's physical needs while teaching them the Word of God. We are currently working on building a new children's home in India and expanding this mission into Pakistan. God has opened remarkable doors in both countries, allowing us to reach the "least of these" with the love of Christ.

In addition to our work in India and Pakistan, we partner with the Roma (Gypsy) people in Romania and are prayerfully building a ministry presence in the UK.

The needs are immense, but we trust that the Lord will provide for all that He has called us to do. As it says in Mark 16:15, "And He said to them, 'Go into all the world and preach the gospel to all creation.'" Wherever He leads, we will follow.

By purchasing our devotionals, you are not only being blessed spiritually, but you are also supporting the mission of Jehovah Jireh Ministries. Your contribution helps us bring the gospel to the nations, and for that, we are both humbled and grateful.

Until He Comes, We Must Go,
Dr. Ralph Jenkins

www.jehovahjirehministries.com

We had the honor of having Pastor Ralph as our Pastor for several years. During that time I would take detailed notes of his easy-to-understand sermons.

This book flows from the Word, throughout the examples, and references he provides. It will be a wonderful tool for the body of Christ to share with others, to remind us of the importance of a strong foundation in Christ, and in His Word. It will be beneficial to a new believer as they begin to learn of and follow Christ.

It is systematically written for easy understanding. We will be purchasing and sharing with others we know.

RORY AND DONNA WARREN

***Foundations of Faith** is truly the best daily devotional I have ever read, and I have read dozens of them. Even though I accepted JESUS as my SAVIOR as a young girl, the clear message of the gospel and our daily walk with JESUS is presented clearly for the new person in CHRIST or the older Christian who needs a fresh look at their daily Christian Walk. This devotional is a must read for the new Christian! Plus, **Foundations of Faith** is great for the older Christian to read often just to be reminded of what we have in JESUS...... and that's Everything!!*

BETH MOORE

***Foundations of Faith** daily devotional book is a very easy read for anyone who picks it up. This book us very organized and easy to follow the ebb and flow of its content. One can know immediately that the author allowed the Holy Spirit to direct the written words. This devotional book is highly recommended for anyone who needs to be lifted and encouraged. It is for anyone who seeks to find peace, joy, love and kindness while finding a new life that will last an eternity. This book will make a great gift for any occasion.*

MIKE FRAZIER, ED.D
DIRECTOR OF SCHOOLS
ETOWAH CITY, TN

*I found **Foundations of Faith** to be a thorough and concise but simple and easy to understand compilation of Christian principles/doctrines. Placed in a devotion format, it is a great review for older Christians and a wonderful resource for new Christians. A comprehensive and fundamental approach to Christianity, it is a great foundation of what being a Christian is all about.*

MARIA RATLIFF

*   **Foundations of Faith** *are a must for new believers. It contains much of the basic doctrines of the Christians Faith. It would be great gift at one's baptism. It would also be a great read for those who have known Christ for a while but don't quite understand the doctrines of the Christian faith. It is the best book I've seen or read for new believers.*

*   **Foundations of Faith** *is concise and to the point, yet it is written in an easily understood vocabulary. We highly recommend **Foundations of Faith** to young and older believers alike.*

BILL & NANCY DEHART

An excellent devotional based on the fundamentals of the Christian faith. It is comprehensive yet easy to understand. This would benefit any Christian no matter where you are in your walk with Christ.

DR. JEFF CARNEY

I first met Ralph Jenkins when he was a 16-year-old student as well as a gifted athlete and leader at Model High School in Rome, GA. He sat in the front of my English class and flashed his winning smile capturing my attention immediately. That sparkling personality is a vital part of his sincere call to winning souls to Christ.

*   *These daily devotions are both authentic and encouraging from this good man who now works so totally dedicated to "GOD'S TEAM."*

*   *This is a **must have** work for both new and seasoned Christians to bolster each day with inspiration and support from **God's Holy Word.***

PRICILLA MORRIS BARNETT
RETIRED TEACHER

*I hope you find this journey with **Foundations of Faith** to be helpful in your everyday walk with Christ. Dr. Jenkins has created a basic study to increase your doctrinal knowledge according to biblical principles. I pray that this study will strengthen your faith and relationship with the Lord Jesus Christ.*

BARRY R. HENDERSON
OWNER – SECOND GENERATION
HENDERSON & SONS FUNERAL HOMES, ROME, GA

FOUNDATIONS

of FAITH

Matthew 7:24: *"Therefore everyone who hears these words of Mine and acts on them, may be compared to a wise man who built his house on the rock"*

DAILY DEVOTIONALS MEANT TO BE BUILDING BLOCKS TO STRENGTHEN AND ENCOURAGE THE LIFE THAT BELONGS TO CHRIST JESUS.

REVIVING THE CHURCH | REACHING THE LOST

JEHOVAH JIREH *Ministries*

THE LORD WHO PROVIDES

First Edition: 2025
Foundations of Faith / Dr. Ralph W. Jenkins
Paperback ISBN: 978-1-958585-96-2
eBook ISBN: 978-1-958585-97-9

CONTENTS

FOUNDATIONS
of FAITH

ACKNOWLEDGMENTS

I would like thank God for my pastor, Dr. Talmadge Barnes. Through his teaching and his actions he taught me trust Jesus above all, to love the Word of God, to pray continually, to love the church and love others without preference.

A true man of God that, though not perfect (for he is a man) I never saw him falter in his faith. I know it was because of his continual diligence in the reading and love of studying God's Word.

To God be the glory and Christ exalted: I am who I am because God placed this man in my life over 40 years ago.

ABOUT THE AUTHOR

Dr. Ralph Jenkins has been a Christian for more than 40 years and has served in full time ministry for 30-plus years. He has spent that time reading, studying, and memorizing God's Word. He has often said, "People don't care what you know until they know that you care."

Dr. Jenkins has pastored four churches and is the founder of Jehovah Jireh Ministries. JJM has a mission to take the gospel to the world, holding crusades and revivals, training pastors, and planting churches among the unreached. He personal motto is Isaiah 6:8-9; *Then I heard the voice of the Lord saying, "Whom shall I send, who will go for us?" Then I said, "Here I am, Send me!"*

Dr. Jenkins has spent over 20 years traveling to Romania, Jamacia, the UK, India, and Pakistan to proclaim the gospel to those who are perishing and to equip and encourage the Christ's beloved church.

His wife Tammy is the heart of it all. Without God putting her in his life over 40 years ago there is no way he would be serving the Lord now. He has said that without a doubt he is one man that married the woman God ordained for him to have from the foundations of the earth. Christ is his first love, and then Tammy. She is his wife, caretaker, secretary and most of all his number-one Prayer Warrior.

He has a daughter and son-in-law, along with two grandchildren. They are also in full time ministry today, pastoring God's church and serving with Ralph & Tammy at Jehovah Jireh Ministries.

PREFACE

Welcome to *Foundations of Faith*, a devotional journey designed to build up, equip, and encourage your faith. Whether you are a new believer just beginning your walk with Christ or someone who has known Him for many years, this devotional is crafted to deepen your understanding of who God is and what it means to follow Him.

A JOURNEY OF FAITH

The Christian life is often described as a journey, a path we walk each day with Jesus by our side. Along this path, we encounter both challenges and joys, uncertainties and assurances. It is a journey that requires faith, trust, and continual growth. The goal of this devotional is to guide you along this journey, helping you to lay a solid foundation of faith, rooted in the unchanging truth of God's Word.

BUILDING ON THE ROCK

Jesus taught about the importance of building our lives on a solid foundation. In Matthew 7:24-25, He said, "Everyone who hears these words of Mine and acts on them may be compared to a wise man who built his house on the rock. And the rain fell, and the floods came, and the winds blew and slammed against that house; and yet it did not fall, for it had been founded on the rock." This devotional is designed to help you build your life on the Rock—Jesus Christ. Each day's reading will bring you deeper into the foundational truths of the Christian faith, helping you to grow in knowledge, wisdom, and love.

FOR NEW BELIEVERS AND SEASONED CHRISTIANS ALIKE

Whether you are new to the faith or have been walking with Jesus for many years, we all need to be reminded of the core truths that define our relationship with God. These truths are not just for beginners; they are the bedrock upon which every believer's life is built. Throughout this 12-week journey we will explore essential doctrines such as the nature of God, salvation by grace, the power of prayer, and living out our faith in everyday life. Each devotion is designed to be relevant and applicable, offering insight, encouragement, and practical steps for spiritual growth.

A SOURCE OF ENCOURAGEMENT

In a world filled with uncertainty and change we need anchors for our souls. My hope is that this devotional will be a source of encouragement, bringing you closer to God and grounding you in His love and truth. As you read, reflect, and pray, may you experience the transforming power of God's Word and the presence of His Spirit. May your faith be strengthened, your heart encouraged, and your life filled with the peace and joy that come from knowing Christ.

WALKING TOGETHER

You are not alone as you embark on this devotional journey. We are all part of the body of Christ, growing together in faith. Use these devotionals as a tool for personal growth, but also consider sharing what you learn with others. Discuss the readings with a friend, join a small group, or use these devotions as a starting point for conversations about faith. The Christian journey is meant to be shared. We grow stronger when we walk together.

A PRAYER FOR YOU

My prayer for you, dear reader, is that through this devotional you will come to know Jesus more deeply and love Him more fully. May your foundation of faith be strengthened, and may your life be a reflection of His grace and truth. May you be built up, equipped, and encouraged in your walk with Christ, and may you find joy in the journey.

In His love,
Dr. Ralph W. Jenkins

DEDICATION

To all those who seek to know God more deeply and follow Jesus more faithfully, this book is dedicated to you.

Whether you are just beginning your journey of faith or have walked with Christ for many years, may these devotionals strengthen your foundation, deepen your understanding, and draw you closer to the heart of God. May you find in these pages the encouragement, guidance, and wisdom you need to grow in grace and truth.

And to my family, for their unwavering support and love. Thank you for encouraging me in my faith and for walking this journey alongside me. Your prayers and presence are a constant source of strength and joy.

— Dr. Ralph W. Jenkins

DR. RALPH W. JENKINS

TO THE READER OF FOUNDATIONS OF FAITH:

First, I want to thank you for picking up this devotional book. Whether you're a new believer just starting your journey with Jesus or someone who has walked with the Lord for years, I believe that God has something special to say to you through these pages. So, let's talk about how to get the most out of this devotional. Imagine I'm right there with you, encouraging you as you hold this book in your hands.

TAKE YOUR TIME

Don't rush through the devotions. Each day is designed to be a moment of pause in your busy life, a time to connect with God and allow Him to speak to your heart. I encourage you to find a quiet place, free from distractions. Maybe it's first thing in the morning, during a lunch break, or before you go to bed. The important thing is that you make this time a priority. Give yourself permission to slow down and absorb what God is saying through His Word.

READ PRAYERFULLY

Before you start reading each devotion, take a moment to pray. Ask God to open your heart and mind to His Word. Pray for understanding and for the Holy Spirit to guide you as you read. This book is more than just words on a page; it's a tool for God to speak into your life. So approach it with an open heart and a prayerful attitude.

FOLLOW ALONG IN YOUR BIBLE

As you read each devotional, you'll find a scripture reading that goes along with it. I want to encourage you to open your Bible and read those passages yourself. There's something powerful about seeing God's Word with your own eyes. Write down any thoughts, questions, or insights that come to mind. Don't worry if you don't understand everything right away. The Bible is a living book, and each time you read it, God can reveal new truths to you.

STUDY AND REFLECT

Each devotion is designed to dig a little deeper into the scripture and help you understand what it means and how it applies to your life. Take time to think about the questions or ideas presented. Reflect on how the message relates to your own experiences. Be honest with yourself and with God. If something challenges you, write it down. If a particular verse or idea stands out, highlight it.

APPLY WHAT YOU LEARN

The real transformation happens when we take what we've read and learned and apply it to our daily lives. At the end of each devotional you'll find a challenge or practical step to take. Don't skip over this part. These challenges are meant to help you live out your faith in a tangible way. Whether it's spending more time in prayer, showing kindness to someone, or stepping out in faith, these actions are where growth happens.

COMMIT TO FOLLOW THROUGH

I know it can be easy to read a devotional, feel encouraged, and then move on without making any changes. I want to encourage you to commit to following through with the daily challenge. Let each devotion be a stepping stone in your journey of faith. God will honor your commitment and faithfulness, and you'll begin to see the fruits of your efforts in your spiritual growth and relationship with Him.

STAY ENCOURAGED

There may be days when you feel like you're not learning anything or when life gets so busy that finding time for devotions seems impossible.

Remember, it's okay. God sees your heart and your efforts. Keep coming back to Him. Even if you miss a day or two, pick up right where you left off. The important thing is to keep moving forward, one step at a time.

FIRMING UP YOUR FAITH

"As you journey through each week's theme, take time to engage with the *"Firming Up Your Foundation"* questions at the end of each week. These questions are designed to deepen your understanding, challenge you to apply what you've learned, and encourage thoughtful reflection on your walk with Christ. Whether used in personal study or group discussions, they serve as building blocks to solidify your foundation of faith."

KNOW THAT I'M PRAYING FOR YOU

Finally, I want you to know that I am praying for you as you go through this devotional. My prayer is that God will use these devotions to strengthen your faith, deepen your understanding of His Word, and draw you closer to Him. I'm standing with you in spirit, cheering you on, and believing that God is going to do amazing things in your life. I pray that each day's devotional will be just what you need for that day.

Thank you again for embarking on this journey with *Foundations of Faith*. I can't wait to see how God moves in your life as you read, follow, study, and apply His Word.

In His love and grace,
Pastor Ralph

AM I SAVED???

It may be that as you start to read this devotional that you are unsure if you are or are not saved. May we present to you the gospel of Christ and how to be saved before you begin.

THE ROMAN ROAD TO SALVATION

SCRIPTURE READING:

- Romans 3:23 (NASB): "For all have sinned and fall short of the glory of God."
- Romans 6:23 (NASB): "For the wages of sin is death, but the gracious gift of God is eternal life in Christ Jesus our Lord."
- Romans 5:8 (NASB): "But God demonstrates His own love toward us, in that while we were still sinners, Christ died for us."
- Romans 10:9-10 (NASB): "That if you confess with your mouth Jesus as Lord, and believe in your heart that God raised Him from the dead, you will be saved; for with the heart a person believes, resulting in righteousness, and with the mouth he confesses, resulting in salvation."
- Romans 10:13 (NASB): "For everyone who calls on the name of the Lord will be saved."

DEVOTION:

The "Romans Road to Salvation" is a powerful and clear presentation of the gospel, drawn from key verses in the book of Romans. It walks us through the steps of recognizing our need for salvation, understanding God's solution, and responding to His offer of eternal life.

STEP 1: OUR CONDITION—ROMANS 3:23

The journey begins with a sobering truth: "For all have sinned and fall short of the glory of God." Every person is born into sin, and no one can measure up to God's perfect standard. This verse eliminates any illusion that we can earn our way to heaven or live a life good enough to merit God's favor. We must first acknowledge our sinful state, our inability to save ourselves.

STEP 2: THE CONSEQUENCE—ROMANS 6:23

Sin comes with a dire consequence: "For the wages of sin is death." Sin leads to spiritual death, a separation from God. But this verse doesn't end with despair; it presents hope: "But the gracious gift of God is eternal life in Christ Jesus our Lord." While our sin earns us death, God's grace offers us eternal life through Jesus. This gift is not something we can achieve; it's something we receive.

STEP 3: GOD'S DEMONSTRATION OF LOVE—ROMANS 5:8

God didn't wait for us to clean up our act. Romans 5:8 declares, "But God demonstrates His own love toward us, in that while we were still sinners, Christ died for us." Jesus' sacrificial death on the cross is the ultimate expression of God's love. He took our place, bore our punishment, and made a way for us to be reconciled with God.

STEP 4: OUR RESPONSE—ROMANS 10:9-10

Salvation requires a personal response: "If you confess with your mouth Jesus as Lord, and believe in your heart that God raised Him from the dead, you will be saved." This verse outlines the simplicity and depth of faith. It's not just intellectual assent; it's a heart-felt belief that transforms your life. Confessing Jesus as Lord means surrendering to His authority and trusting in His resurrection as the cornerstone of your faith.

STEP 5: ASSURANCE OF SALVATION—ROMANS 10:13

The journey concludes with a promise: "For everyone who calls on the name of the Lord will be saved." This is the assurance we have in Christ—no one who sincerely seeks Him will be turned away. God's offer of salvation is open to all, regardless of background, past sins, or present circumstances.

REFLECTION:

As you reflect on these verses, consider where you are on this journey. Have you acknowledged your need for salvation? Have you received God's gift of eternal life? If you've already walked this road, take the time to thank God today for your salvation.

Ask Him: who in your life needs to hear the Gospel of Christ? The Romans Road is not just a path to personal salvation; it's a guide we can share with others who are seeking the truth. Just pass this message along to them.

If today you realize your need to be saved and can believe with all your heart that Jesus died for your sins and God raised Him from the dead then we invite you to say, from the heart, this prayer.

PRAYER:

Heavenly Father, I know I have sinned and come short of what you expect of me. I know I need salvation. Today, I confess Christ as my Lord. I believe Jesus died for my sins and rose from the grave. According to your holy Word, if I confess with my mouth and believe with my heart in Christ Jesus then I am saved. I thank you for saving me and I ask you to lead me now and help me live the life you have called me to. In Jesus Name, Amen.

If you said this prayer (confessed with your mouth), believing in your heart that God raised Jesus from the dead then according to God's Word you are now saved.

Please send us note at info@jehovahjirehministries.com and let us know of your decision.

WEEK 1
SALVATION

DAY 1: THE GIFT OF GRACE

DAY 2: FAITH IN JESUS

DAY 3: REPENTANCE AND FORGIVENESS

DAY 4: THE ASSURANCE OF SALVATION

DAY 5: THE NEW BIRTH

DAY 6: JUSTIFICATION BY FAITH

DAY 7: LIVING IN THE NEW IDENTITY

DAY 1: THE GIFT OF GRACE

Scripture: Ephesians 2:8-9 (NASB)
*"For by grace you have been saved through faith; and
that not of yourselves, it is the gift of God; not as a result of works, so that no one may boast."*

ANECDOTE:

Imagine a person who receives a surprise invitation to a luxurious
banquet. This person has no wealth, no fine clothes, and no means to
repay the host. Yet, the invitation says, "Come as you are. Everything
has been prepared for you." With a hesitant heart, this person arrives at
the banquet hall and is welcomed with open arms. All the finest foods
and drinks are freely offered, and a beautiful robe is placed upon their
shoulders. The host says, "You are my honored guest. Enjoy everything
without cost, for I have paid the price."

APPLICATION:

This story illustrates the nature of God's grace. Grace is God's unmer-
ited favor; it is His goodness given to us without us deserving it. Salvation
is offered to us not because we have earned it through good deeds, moral
living, or religious rituals, but purely because of God's grace. The Bible
tells us that all have sinned and fall short of the glory of God (Romans
3:23). Our sin separates us from God, and no amount of good works can
bridge that gap. But through Jesus Christ, God provided the way for us
to be reconciled to Him. This reconciliation is a gift—freely given, yet
infinitely valuable.

The Apostle Paul reminds us that it is by grace we are saved, through
faith, and not by our works. This truth humbles us, reminding us that
we cannot boast about our salvation as if we had earned it. Instead, we
should be filled with gratitude and worship, knowing that God has lav-
ished His love upon us. This grace motivates us to live differently, not to

try to earn God's favor, but because we have already received it. Grace changes our hearts, transforms our desires, and compels us to extend that same grace to others.

FURTHER SCRIPTURE:

- Titus 3:4-7: Emphasizes the kindness and love of God, not by works but by His mercy.
- Romans 11:6: Highlights that if salvation is by grace, it cannot be based on works.
- 2 Timothy 1:9: God saved us and called us to a holy life, not because of anything we have done but because of His own purpose and grace.

PRAYER:

Heavenly Father, I am in awe of Your grace. Thank You for saving me, not because of anything I have done, but because of Your great love and mercy. Help me to live each day in the reality of Your grace, extending it to others and growing in my faith. May my life reflect Your goodness and lead others to see the beauty of Your grace. Amen.

PERSONAL REFLECTION:

How does the understanding that salvation is a gift of grace change my approach to God and to others today? What can I do to show gratitude for God's grace in my daily life?

DAY 2: FAITH IN JESUS

Scripture: John 3:16 (NASB)
*"For God so loved the world, that He gave His
only begotten Son, that whoever believes in Him
shall not perish, but have eternal life."*

ANECDOTE:

Think of a trust fall exercise, where a person stands with their back to a group of friends and then falls, trusting that they will catch him. The person falling doesn't see the arms ready to catch him, but he believes and falls back with confidence. His trust is not in what he sees but in the word and reliability of his friends.

APPLICATION:

Faith in Jesus is like that trust fall. It means believing in what we cannot see and trusting in the promises of God. In John 3:16, Jesus explains the depth of God's love: He gave His only Son so that whoever believes in Him will not perish but have eternal life. This is the core of the gospel message—God's love and our response to it through faith. Faith is not merely intellectual agreement but involves trust and reliance on Jesus for our salvation. It's a complete surrender to Him, recognizing that He alone is the way, the truth, and the life (John 14:6).

Faith in Jesus means we rely not on our own understanding or efforts but trust fully in what Jesus accomplished on the cross. Through His death and resurrection, Jesus paid the penalty for our sins, defeated death, and offers us eternal life. Our faith, though sometimes small and imperfect, connects us to the perfect Savior. It's like the roots of a tree that, though unseen, hold the tree steady and draw nourishment. When our faith is in Jesus, we are rooted in Him, and He becomes our source of strength, hope, and salvation.

FURTHER SCRIPTURE:

- Romans 10:9-10: Confessing Jesus as Lord and believing in His resurrection leads to salvation.
- Hebrews 11:1: Faith is being sure of what we hope for and certain of what we do not see.
- John 20:29: Jesus blesses those who have not seen and yet have believed.

PRAYER:

Lord Jesus, I place my faith in You. I believe that You are the Son of God who died for my sins and rose again to give me eternal life. Help me to trust You more each day, even when I cannot see the way ahead. Strengthen my faith and let it be a testimony to Your saving grace. Amen.

PERSONAL REFLECTION:

In what areas of my life do I need to trust Jesus more fully? How can I grow in my faith and reliance on Him today?

DAY 3: REPENTANCE AND FORGIVENESS

Scripture: Acts 3:19 (NASB)
"Therefore repent and return, so that your sins may be wiped away, in order that times of refreshing may come from the presence of the Lord."

ANECDOTE:

Imagine a river that becomes polluted by waste and toxins, making the water undrinkable and harmful to all life around it. A group of people comes along and begins the process of cleaning the river, removing the toxins and restoring it to its pure state. Once clean, the river becomes a source of life and refreshment again.

APPLICATION:

Repentance is the process of cleaning the river of our hearts. It involves recognizing that we have sinned against God and turning away from those sins. Repentance is more than feeling sorry; it's a change of mind and heart that leads to a change in action. When Peter called people to repent in Acts 3:19, he was inviting them to experience the forgiveness of God, which wipes away sins and brings refreshment to the soul.

True repentance is like the first step in a journey back to God. It acknowledges that our way leads to destruction, and it chooses God's way instead. This repentance opens the door for forgiveness, as God promises to cleanse us from all unrighteousness when we confess our sins (1 John 1:9). The refreshing presence of the Lord comes into our lives when we repent, bringing healing, peace, and restoration. Just as a clean river brings life to everything around it, a repentant heart opens the way for God's life-giving Spirit to flow in and through us.

FURTHER SCRIPTURE:

- Psalm 51:10: David's prayer for a clean heart and a right spirit.
- Isaiah 55:7: Encouragement to return to the Lord and receive His abundant pardon.
- Luke 15:7: Heaven rejoices over one sinner who repents.

PRAYER:

Heavenly Father, I come to You in repentance, acknowledging my sins and turning away from them. Please forgive me and cleanse me from all unrighteousness. Let Your refreshing presence fill my heart and lead me in Your ways. Thank You for Your mercy and grace. Amen.

PERSONAL REFLECTION:

Is there any area of my life where I need to repent and turn back to God? How can I experience God's refreshing presence today?

DAY 4: THE ASSURANCE OF SALVATION

Scripture: Romans 8:38-39 (NASB)

"For I am convinced that neither death, nor life, nor angels, nor principalities, nor things present, nor things to come, nor powers, nor height, nor depth, nor any other created thing, will be able to separate us from the love of God, which is in Christ Jesus our Lord."

ANECDOTE:

A young child clutches a teddy bear tightly while navigating through a dark room. Despite the darkness and fear, the child feels comforted by the familiarity and safety the teddy bear provides. Even when unseen dangers lurk, the child knows it is safe because of the security of holding onto the bear.

APPLICATION:

As believers, our assurance of salvation is much more secure than a child's hold on a teddy bear. It is not based on feelings or circumstances but on the unchanging love and promises of God. Paul's declaration in Romans 8:38-39 is a powerful reminder that nothing—absolutely nothing—can separate us from the love of God that is in Christ Jesus. This assurance provides us with a firm foundation even when we face doubts, fears, or challenges.

Understanding this truth brings peace and security. Our salvation is not fragile; it is anchored in God's love and secured by the work of Jesus on the cross. Knowing that God's love for us is unwavering gives us confidence to face life's storms. It encourages us to persevere in faith, even when we don't understand what's happening around us. Assurance of salvation is not a license to live carelessly but a motivation to live boldly for Christ, knowing that we are loved, forgiven, and held securely by Him.

FURTHER SCRIPTURE:

- John 10:28-29: Jesus assures us that no one can snatch believers out of His hand.
- Philippians 1:6: God will complete the good work He began in us.
- 1 John 5:13: Assurance of eternal life for those who believe in the Son of God.

PRAYER:

Lord, thank You for the assurance of Your love and my salvation. Help me to trust in Your promises and rest in the security that nothing can separate me from You. May this assurance fill me with courage and joy as I live for You each day. Amen.

PERSONAL REFLECTION:

How does the assurance of God's love and my salvation give me peace today? What can I do to live more boldly in light of this truth?

DAY 5: THE NEW BIRTH

Scripture: John 3:3 (NASB)
"Jesus answered and said to him, 'Truly, truly, I say to you, unless one is born again he cannot see the kingdom of God.'"

ANECDOTE:

A caterpillar spends its life crawling on the ground, limited by its form and nature. But after a transformative process inside a cocoon, it emerges as a butterfly, able to fly and see the world from a new perspective. The butterfly's life is entirely different from its former existence; it has been made new.

APPLICATION:

The new birth Jesus speaks of is a spiritual transformation that changes our nature and our destiny. Being born again means more than just adopting a new set of beliefs; it means receiving a new life from God. Our old self, with its sinful nature and desires, is put to death, and we are made new by the power of the Holy Spirit. This new birth brings us into a living relationship with God and opens our eyes to His kingdom.

When we are born again, we begin to see the world through God's eyes. Our values, priorities, and desires are transformed. We no longer live for ourselves but for Christ, who gave His life for us. This transformation is not something we achieve on our own; it is the work of God's Spirit in us. Just as a butterfly cannot return to being a caterpillar, we are called to live out our new identity in Christ, growing in holiness and reflecting God's love.

FURTHER SCRIPTURE:

- 2 Corinthians 5:17: In Christ, we are new creations; the old has gone, and the new has come.
- 1 Peter 1:23: We are born again through the living and enduring word of God.
- Titus 3:5: God saved us through the washing of rebirth and renewal by the Holy Spirit.

PRAYER:

Lord, thank You for giving me new life through Jesus. Help me to live as a new creation, growing closer to You and reflecting Your love and holiness in all I do. May my life be a testimony of Your transforming power. Amen.

PERSONAL REFLECTION:

How does my new birth in Christ change the way I live today? What areas of my life need to reflect more of my new identity in Christ?

DAY 6: JUSTIFICATION BY FAITH

Scripture: Romans 5:1 (NASB)
*"Therefore, having been justified by faith, we have
peace with God through our Lord Jesus Christ."*

ANECDOTE:

Imagine a courtroom where a person stands accused of serious
crimes. Evidence against them is overwhelming, and they know they deserve punishment. Then, the judge declares them "not guilty" because
someone else has stepped forward to take the punishment on their behalf. The accused walks out free, overwhelmed with gratitude and a renewed sense of life.

APPLICATION:

Justification is a legal term that means to be declared righteous. In
God's courtroom, we stand guilty because of our sin, deserving of judgment. But because of Jesus' sacrificial death, we are declared not guilty
when we put our faith in Him. Our sins are forgiven, and we are clothed
in Christ's righteousness. This is the essence of justification by faith.

This doctrine is foundational to our peace with God. Without justification, we remain under condemnation. But through faith in Jesus, we
are reconciled to God. We no longer fear judgment because our sins have
been dealt with at the cross. This peace is not just the absence of conflict
but the presence of harmony, knowing that our relationship with God
has been restored. Justification changes our status before God and transforms our daily lives, leading us to live in gratitude, obedience, and love.

FURTHER SCRIPTURE:

- Galatians 2:16: Justification is not by works of the law but by faith in Jesus Christ.
- Romans 3:28: We are justified by faith apart from works of the law.
- Philippians 3:9: Righteousness comes through faith in Christ, not from the law.

PRAYER:

Lord, thank You for justifying me through faith in Jesus. Help me to live in the peace and freedom that comes from knowing I am forgiven and accepted by You. May my life reflect Your righteousness and bring glory to Your name. Amen.

PERSONAL REFLECTION:

How does understanding justification by faith give me peace? How can I live out my gratitude for being justified in my daily life?

DAY 7: LIVING IN THE NEW IDENTITY

Scripture: 2 Corinthians 5:17 (NASB)
"Therefore if anyone is in Christ, he is a new creature; the old things passed away; behold, new things have come."

ANECDOTE:

A sculptor begins with a rough block of stone, seeing a beautiful statue within it. With each careful strike of the chisel, the unnecessary parts are removed, revealing the masterpiece hidden inside. The sculptor's vision guides the entire process, transforming the stone into a work of art.

APPLICATION:

As believers, we are God's workmanship, created anew in Christ Jesus (Ephesians 2:10). Our new identity means that the old ways of living—defined by sin, guilt, and shame—are gone. We are now God's children, loved, forgiven, and called to reflect His character. This transformation is ongoing, like the sculptor shaping the stone. God is continually at work in us, molding us to be more like Jesus.

Living in our new identity means embracing the reality that we are no longer who we used to be. It's easy to fall back into old habits or believe lies about our worth and identity. But God's Word reminds us that we are new creations, with a new purpose and a new destiny. We are called to live in this truth daily, allowing God's Spirit to shape our thoughts, actions, and desires. This new identity gives us the courage to leave the past behind and walk confidently into the future God has prepared for us.

FURTHER SCRIPTURE:

- Colossians 3:9-10: We have put off the old self
  and put on the new self, which is being renewed in
  knowledge.
- Ephesians 4:22-24: We are to put off the old self
  and put on the new self, created to be like God in
  true righteousness and holiness.
- Romans 6:4: We are to walk in newness of life,
  just as Christ was raised from the dead.

PRAYER:

Father, thank You for making me a new creation in Christ. Help me to live out my new identity each day, leaving behind the old ways and embracing the new life You have given me. May my life be a reflection of Your love, holiness, and grace. Amen.

PERSONAL REFLECTION:

What does my new identity in Christ mean for how I live today? Are there old habits or mindsets I need to leave behind to fully embrace who I am in Christ?

FIRMING UP YOUR FOUNDATION
SALVATION

- What does the concept of grace mean to you, and how have you experienced it in your life?

- How has your understanding of faith in Jesus deepened through this week's devotions?

- Reflect on the assurance of salvation. How does it impact your daily life and decisions?

- What does living in your new identity in Christ mean for you personally?

- Who can you share the message of salvation with, and how might you approach it?

WEEK TWO
THE NATURE OF GOD

DAY 8: GOD THE CREATOR - GENESIS 1:1

DAY 9: THE TRINITY: ONE GOD
IN THREE PERSONS –

MATTHEW 28:19

DAY 10: GOD'S OMNIPOTENCE
- JEREMIAH 32:17

DAY 11: GOD'S OMNISCIENCE
- PSALM 139:1-4

DAY 12: GOD'S OMNIPRESENCE
- PSALM 139:7-10

DAY 13: THE HOLINESS OF
GOD - ISAIAH 6

DAY 14: GOD'S LOVE - 1 JOHN 4:16

DAY 8: GOD THE CREATOR

Scripture: Genesis 1:1 (NASB)
"In the beginning God created the heavens and the earth."

ANECDOTE:

Imagine a master artist who envisions a beautiful painting. With every brushstroke, the painting comes to life, filled with vibrant colors and intricate details. People marvel at the finished masterpiece, admiring its beauty and the skill of the artist. Yet, the artist's joy is not just in the painting itself but in the ability to share his vision and creativity with the world.

APPLICATION:

God, as the Creator, is the ultimate master artist. In the opening verse of the Bible, we see God's powerful act of creation: "In the beginning, God created the heavens and the earth." Everything that exists originated from Him. The vast expanse of the universe, the complexity of life, and the beauty of nature are all His handiwork. This truth has profound implications for us. Firstly, it means that God is sovereign. As Creator, He has authority over all things. Nothing is outside His control, and everything finds its purpose and meaning in Him.

Secondly, recognizing God as Creator helps us see our own value and purpose. We are not accidents or the result of random chance; we are intentionally designed by a loving Creator. Psalm 139:14 reminds us that we are "fearfully and wonderfully made." This means that each of us has intrinsic worth and significance. Understanding this should lead us to worship, humility, and a desire to know God more deeply. It also gives us a sense of responsibility to care for God's creation, recognizing it as a reflection of His glory.

FURTHER SCRIPTURE:

- Psalm 19:1: The heavens declare the glory of God, the skies proclaim the work of His hands.
- Isaiah 40:28: God is the everlasting Creator who does not grow tired or weary.
- Colossians 1:16: All things were created by Him and for Him.

PRAYER:

Creator God, I stand in awe of Your power and majesty. Thank You for the beauty of creation and for making me in Your image. Help me to see Your hand in everything around me and to honor You in the way I live. May I appreciate and care for the world You have made, and may my life reflect Your creative love. Amen.

PERSONAL REFLECTION:

How does recognizing God as my Creator change the way I see myself and the world around me? What are some ways I can honor God through His creation today?

DAY 9: THE TRINITY: ONE GOD IN THREE PERSONS

Scripture: Matthew 28:19 (NASB)
"Go therefore and make disciples of all the nations, baptizing them in the name of the Father and the Son and the Holy Spirit."

ANECDOTE:

Consider a triangle, a simple shape with three sides and three angles. Each side is distinct, yet together they form one complete shape. If one side were removed, the triangle would no longer exist. The triangle's completeness relies on all three sides being present.

APPLICATION:

The concept of the Trinity—one God in three persons: Father, Son, and Holy Spirit—is foundational to the Christian faith, though it can be challenging to understand fully. Each Person of the Trinity is distinct, yet all are one in essence and purpose. God the Father is the creator and sustainer of all things. Jesus, the Son, is God in the flesh, who came to redeem humanity through His death and resurrection. The Holy Spirit is God's presence within us, guiding, comforting, and empowering believers.

While the term "Trinity" is not found in the Bible, the concept is clearly present. In Matthew 28:19, Jesus commands His disciples to baptize in the name (singular) of the Father, Son, and Holy Spirit, indicating the unity and diversity within the Godhead. The Trinity is a mystery that shows us the relational nature of God. He exists in perfect unity and love within Himself. This understanding impacts our lives profoundly. It shows us that God is inherently relational, inviting us into a relationship with Him and with others. It also means that our salvation and sanctification involve all three Persons of the Trinity working together.

FURTHER SCRIPTURE:

- 2 Corinthians 13:14: The grace of Jesus, the love of God, and the fellowship of the Holy Spirit.
- John 14:16-17: Jesus speaks of sending the Holy Spirit, another Helper.
- Genesis 1:26: "Let us make man in our image," reflecting the plurality of the Godhead.

PRAYER:

Father, Son, and Holy Spirit, I worship You as the one true God. Thank You for the love and unity within Yourself that overflows into my life. Help me to understand more of who You are and to live in a way that reflects Your love and truth. May I grow in my relationship with You and others, knowing that I am made in the image of a relational God. Amen.

PERSONAL REFLECTION:

How does understanding God as Trinity deepen my relationship with Him? How can I reflect the love and unity of the Trinity in my relationships with others.

DAY 10: GOD'S OMNIPOTENCE

Scripture: Jeremiah 32:17 (NASB)
"Ah, Lord God! Behold, You have made the heavens and the earth by Your great power and by Your outstretched arm! Nothing is too difficult for You."

ANECDOTE:

A child watches in amazement as a construction worker uses a massive crane to lift a heavy beam high in the air. To the child, the beam seemed impossible to move, yet the crane lifted it effortlessly. The child learns that with the right power, even the heaviest loads can be moved.

APPLICATION:

God's omnipotence means that He is all-powerful. There is nothing too difficult for Him. He created the universe with a word, parted the Red Sea, and raised Jesus from the dead. His power is limitless and beyond our comprehension. Jeremiah's declaration in Jeremiah 32:17 reminds us of this truth: "Nothing is too difficult for You." This assurance of God's omnipotence is a source of comfort and confidence for believers.

Knowing that God is all-powerful means that no situation is beyond His ability to handle. When we face trials, challenges, or seemingly impossible circumstances, we can trust that God is able to do what we cannot. His power is not just a force but is combined with His wisdom, love, and sovereignty. Therefore, we can rely on Him not only to act, but to act in the best way possible for His glory and our good.

This understanding also challenges us to live in faith, not in fear. We are called to trust God's power, even when we don't see the immediate results we desire. His timing and methods may be different from ours, but His power is always at work. Knowing this should lead us to worship and surrender, acknowledging that God is in control and that His power is sufficient for every need.

FURTHER SCRIPTURE:

- Psalm 147:5: God's understanding is infinite, and His power is great.
- Ephesians 3:20: God is able to do far more abundantly than all we ask or think.
- Luke 1:37: Nothing will be impossible with God.

PRAYER:

Almighty God, I praise You for Your great power. Nothing is too difficult for You. Help me to trust in Your strength, especially when I feel weak or helpless. May I rely on Your power in my daily life, knowing that You are able to handle every situation I face. Thank You for being my refuge and strength. Amen.

PERSONAL REFLECTION:

What challenges am I facing that I need to trust God's power to handle? How can I live with greater faith, knowing that nothing is too difficult for Him?

DAY 11: GOD'S OMNISCIENCE

Scripture: Psalm 139:1-4 (NASB)
*"O Lord, You have searched me and known me. You know when
I sit down and when I rise up; You understand my thought
from afar. You scrutinize my path and my lying down, and
are intimately acquainted with all my ways. Even before there
is a word on my tongue, behold, O Lord, You know it all."*

ANECDOTE:

A librarian can find any book in the library because he or she knows the layout of every shelf and catalog. They can tell you where to find information, down to the exact page number. Their knowledge of the library is complete, allowing them to guide others with confidence.

APPLICATION:

God's omniscience means that He knows everything: past, present, and future. He knows every detail of the universe, every thought in our minds, every word on our tongues before we speak it. David's words in Psalm 139:1-4 express awe at God's complete knowledge of him. God is not distant or uninvolved; He is intimately acquainted with all our ways.

This truth can be both comforting and convicting. Comforting, because it means we are never alone or misunderstood. God knows us better than we know ourselves and loves us deeply. Convicting, because it means we cannot hide from God. Our thoughts, motives, and actions are all laid bare before Him. This should lead us to live transparently, seeking to please God in all we do, knowing that nothing escapes His notice. God's omniscience also means that He knows the best path for our lives. When we face uncertainty or confusion, we can trust His guidance. He sees the whole picture, whereas we only see a part. Trusting in His knowledge gives us peace and direction, knowing that His plans for us are good.

FURTHER SCRIPTURE:

- Isaiah 46:9-10: God declares the end from the beginning and knows what is to come.
- Hebrews 4:13: Nothing is hidden from God's sight; everything is uncovered before Him.
- Proverbs 15:3: The eyes of the Lord are in every place, watching the evil and the good.

PRAYER:

All-knowing God, I am amazed at Your complete knowledge of me and all creation. Thank You for knowing me fully and still loving me. Help me to live transparently before You, trusting in Your wisdom and guidance. May Your knowledge lead me to greater trust and obedience in my life. Amen.

PERSONAL REFLECTION:

How does knowing that God knows everything about me bring comfort and challenge me? In what areas of my life do I need to trust His wisdom and knowledge more?

DAY 12: GOD'S OMNIPRESENCE

Scripture: Psalm 139:7-10 (NASB)

"Where can I go from Your Spirit? Or where can I flee from Your presence? If I ascend to heaven, You are there; if I make my bed in Sheol, behold, You are there. If I take the wings of the dawn, if I dwell in the remotest part of the sea, even there Your hand will lead me, and Your right hand will lay hold of me."

ANECDOTE:

A child playing hide-and-seek believes they've found the perfect hiding spot. Yet, no matter how well they hide, their parent always finds them. The parent's loving eyes are always on their child, ensuring their safety even during play.

APPLICATION:

God's omnipresence means He is present everywhere at all times. There is no place in the universe where God is not. David's words in Psalm 139 express this reality beautifully: no matter where he goes, God is there. This truth brings great comfort, knowing that we are never alone. In our darkest moments, God is with us. In our greatest joys, He is there, too. His presence is not just a fact; it is a source of strength and guidance. "Even there Your hand will lead me," David says. God's presence means we can face any situation without fear, knowing He is by our side.

God's omnipresence also means we cannot escape Him. Sometimes, like Adam and Eve in the garden, we may want to hide from God because of our sin or guilt. But hiding is impossible. God's presence is constant, and His love is unrelenting. Instead of hiding, we are invited to come to Him, confess our sins, and find forgiveness and grace. God's presence is not meant to be a threat but a source of peace and assurance. It calls us to live in awareness of His nearness, to seek Him in prayer, and to trust that He is always with us.

FURTHER SCRIPTURE:

- Jeremiah 23:23-24: God fills heaven and earth; no one can hide from Him.
- Matthew 28:20: Jesus promises to be with us always, to the end of the age.
- Hebrews 13:5: God promises never to leave us nor forsake us.

PRAYER:

Ever-present God, I thank You that You are always with me. In every situation, I can trust that You are near, guiding, comforting, and protecting me. Help me to live in constant awareness of Your presence and to find my peace and strength in You. May Your presence give me courage and hope, knowing that I am never alone. Amen.

PERSONAL REFLECTION:

How does knowing God is always with me affect my attitude and actions? In what ways can I cultivate a greater awareness of His presence in my daily life?

DAY 13: THE HOLINESS OF GOD

Scripture: Isaiah 6:3 (NASB)
"And one called out to another and said, 'Holy, Holy, Holy,
is the Lord of hosts, The whole earth is full of His glory.'"

ANECDOTE:

Imagine entering a grand cathedral, filled with intricate stained-glass windows that shine with radiant light. As you walk in, you are struck by the silence and the sense of reverence that fills the air. It's a place set apart, where the ordinary world feels distant, and the sacredness of the space draws you into awe and respect.

APPLICATION:

Holiness is one of the defining attributes of God. To say God is holy means He is set apart, pure, and without any flaw or imperfection. In Isaiah 6:3, the seraphim declare God's holiness three times, emphasizing the absolute purity and majesty of God. His holiness is so overwhelming that it fills the whole earth with His glory. God's holiness sets Him apart from all creation, and it is the standard by which all moral purity is measured.

Understanding God's holiness should lead us to reverence and worship. When we recognize how pure and perfect God is, we see our own sinfulness more clearly. Like Isaiah, who cried, "Woe is me!" when he saw God's holiness, we realize our need for God's cleansing and forgiveness. God's holiness also calls us to live differently. 1 Peter 1:15-16 urges us to be holy in all our conduct because God is holy. This doesn't mean we can be perfect in our own strength, but it does mean we strive to live in a way that honors God, relying on His Spirit to transform us.

FURTHER SCRIPTURE:

- 1 Peter 1:15-16: We are called to be holy because God is holy.
- Revelation 4:8: The four living creatures never stop declaring God's holiness.
- Exodus 15:11: God's holiness is unmatched, and He is glorious in His deeds.

PRAYER:

Holy God, I stand in awe of Your purity and perfection. You are set apart, and there is none like You. Forgive me for the ways I have fallen short of Your holiness, and cleanse me with Your grace. Help me to live a life that reflects Your holiness, set apart for Your purposes. May my life bring glory to Your name. Amen.

PERSONAL REFLECTION:

How does God's holiness affect my understanding of His character? What areas of my life need to change to reflect His holiness more fully?

DAY 14: GOD'S LOVE

Scripture: 1 John 4:16 (NASB)
*"We have come to know and have believed the love which
God has for us. God is love, and the one who abides
in love abides in God, and God abides in him."*

ANECDOTE:

A parent lovingly cares for their child, sacrificing sleep and time to ensure the child's well-being. The child may not fully understand the depth of the parent's love, but they feel secure and cherished because of it. The parent's love is constant, even when the child makes mistakes or disobeys.

APPLICATION:

God's love is one of the most profound and comforting truths we can know. The Apostle John declares that "God is love," meaning that love is not just something God does—it's who He is. His love is perfect, unconditional, and unchanging. He loves us not because of what we have done but because of who He is. This love was most clearly demonstrated through Jesus Christ, who laid down His life for us while we were still sinners (Romans 5:8). God's love is not a mere feeling; it is active, sacrificial, and purposeful.

Knowing that God is love gives us confidence and security. We can rest in His love, knowing that nothing can separate us from it (Romans 8:38-39). This truth should shape our identity and influence how we live. When we abide in God's love, we are called to love others in the same way. Our love for others becomes a reflection of God's love for us. Even when we face difficulties, failures, or rejection, we can hold onto the assurance that God's love remains constant. His love gives us the strength to persevere, forgive, and extend grace to others.

FURTHER SCRIPTURE:

- John 3:16: God's love is shown in the giving of His Son for our salvation.
- Romans 8:38-39: Nothing can separate us from the love of God in Christ Jesus.
- 1 John 4:10: Love is defined by God's action of sending His Son to be the propitiation for our sins.

PRAYER:

Loving God, thank You for Your unconditional love. Help me to truly believe and receive Your love every day. May Your love transform my heart and guide my actions. Teach me to love others as You have loved me, and may my life be a testimony of Your love to the world. Amen.

PERSONAL REFLECTION:

How does knowing that God is love change the way I see myself and others? What are some practical ways I can show God's love to those around me today?

FIRMING UP YOUR FOUNDATION
THE NATURE OF GOD

- How does recognizing God as the Creator impact the way you view the world and your role in it?

- What new insights did you gain about the Trinity this week?

- Reflect on God's omnipotence, omniscience, and omnipresence. How do these attributes affect your trust in Him?

- How has this week's focus on God's holiness and love influenced your relationship with Him?

- What steps can you take to honor God's nature in your everyday actions?

WEEK 3
JESUS CHRIST

DAY 15: THE INCARNATION: GOD BECOMING MAN

Scripture: John 1:14 (NASB)
"And the Word became flesh, and dwelt among us, and we saw His glory, glory as of the only begotten from the Father, full of grace and truth."

ANECDOTE:

A young prince, destined to inherit a vast kingdom, decided to disguise himself as a commoner. He lived among his people, experiencing their joys and hardships firsthand. He did this to understand them better and to show them that their ruler cared deeply about their daily lives. The prince's presence among the people transformed how they saw their kingdom and their future.

APPLICATION:

The incarnation of Jesus is a central and transformative truth of the Christian faith. When John writes, "The Word became flesh and dwelt among us," he is expressing the profound mystery that God Himself took on human form. Jesus, the eternal Word, who was with God and was God (John 1:1), became a man to live among His creation. This act was not only an expression of God's love but also a way for Him to identify with us in our humanity. Jesus experienced hunger, pain, sorrow, and joy—He walked the same paths we walk, yet without sin.

The incarnation shows us that God is not distant or removed from our struggles. He understands our pain because He experienced it Himself. This knowledge should bring us immense comfort. When we go through difficulties, we can turn to Jesus, knowing that He empathizes with us and has compassion for our situation. Moreover, the incarnation is the foundation for our salvation. Only by becoming fully human could Jesus become the perfect sacrifice for our sins, bridging the gap between a holy God and sinful humanity. The incarnation invites us into a relationship with a God who is both transcendent and immanent—great and majestic yet intimately involved in our lives.

FURTHER SCRIPTURE:

- Philippians 2:6-8: Jesus, being in very nature God, humbled Himself by becoming human and dying on the cross.
- Hebrews 4:15: Jesus, our High Priest, can sympathize with our weaknesses.
- Isaiah 7:14: Prophecy of the virgin birth of Immanuel, "God with us."

PRAYER:

Heavenly Father, thank You for sending Your Son, Jesus, to dwell among us. Thank You, Jesus, for becoming human, experiencing our world, and showing us the depth of Your love. Help me to live in awe of the incarnation and to find comfort in knowing that You understand my struggles. May Your presence in my life transform me daily. Amen.

PERSONAL REFLECTION:

How does understanding the incarnation of Jesus change my view of God? What are some ways I can draw near to Jesus, knowing He understands my humanity?

DAY 16: THE SINLESS LIFE OF CHRIST

Scripture: 1 Peter 2:22 (NASB)
"He committed no sin, nor was any deceit found in His mouth."

ANECDOTE:

Imagine a pure white sheet hanging on a clothesline. Over time, dust, dirt, and stains accumulate, making the once pristine sheet look dingy. No matter how hard you try to clean it, it never looks perfectly white again. But Jesus' life was like a sheet that remained untouched by any stain, always pure and spotless.

APPLICATION:

Jesus' sinless life is a foundational aspect of His identity and His mission. Unlike all other human beings, Jesus lived a life free from sin. He was tempted in every way that we are, yet He did not give in to sin (Hebrews 4:15). This perfection in thought, word, and deed made Him the only acceptable sacrifice for our sins. As the spotless Lamb of God, Jesus could take upon Himself the sins of the world, offering Himself as a perfect sacrifice that satisfied God's justice and demonstrated His love.

Understanding Jesus' sinless life helps us to see the standard of holiness that God requires. It also shows us that Jesus is not just an example to follow, but a Savior to rely on. We all fall short of the glory of God (Romans 3:23), and we cannot achieve sinlessness on our own. But because Jesus lived a perfect life and died in our place, we can be forgiven and receive His righteousness. This truth should lead us to humility and gratitude. It should also encourage us to strive for holiness, empowered by the Holy Spirit, knowing that Jesus' life is the model we aim to follow.

FURTHER SCRIPTURE:

- 2 Corinthians 5:21: Jesus, who knew no sin, became sin for us so that we might become the righteousness of God.
- Hebrews 7:26: Jesus is holy, blameless, pure, set apart from sinners.
- John 8:46: Jesus challenges His accusers to find any sin in Him, and they cannot.

PRAYER:

Lord Jesus, thank You for living a sinless life and offering Yourself as the perfect sacrifice for my sins. I acknowledge my need for Your righteousness and forgiveness. Help me to follow Your example and live a life that honors You. Empower me by Your Spirit to overcome temptation and to grow in holiness each day. Amen.

PERSONAL REFLECTION:

How does knowing that Jesus was sinless impact my view of Him as my Savior? In what areas of my life do I need to strive for greater holiness, following Jesus' example?

DAY 17: JESUS, THE GOOD SHEPHERD

Scripture: John 10:11 (NASB)
*"I am the good shepherd; the good shep-
herd lays down His life for the sheep."*

ANECDOTE:

A shepherd watches over his flock, leading them to green pastures and fresh water. He knows each sheep by name and is attentive to every need. When danger comes, the shepherd stands between the sheep and the threat, protecting them even at the risk of his own life. The sheep feel safe and cared for because they trust the shepherd's voice and guidance.

APPLICATION:

Jesus' declaration, "I am the good shepherd" is rich with meaning and comfort. In biblical times, a shepherd's role was to guide, protect, and provide for the sheep. Jesus, as our Good Shepherd, does all these things and more. He knows each of us personally, calls us by name, and leads us in paths of righteousness. Unlike a hired hand, Jesus is committed to His sheep to the point of laying down His life for them. This is exactly what He did on the cross, sacrificing Himself so that we might have life.

Knowing Jesus as our Good Shepherd means we can trust Him completely. He sees the dangers we cannot see and is always working for our good. Even when we face trials or walk through dark valleys, we can have peace, knowing that Jesus is with us, guiding and protecting us. His voice is our guide, and we learn to recognize it by spending time in His Word and in prayer. The Good Shepherd's care is constant, and His love is sacrificial. This should give us confidence and security, knowing that we are deeply loved and always under His watchful care.

FURTHER SCRIPTURE:

- Psalm 23: The Lord is my shepherd; I shall not want.
- Isaiah 40:11: God tends His flock like a shepherd, gathering the lambs in His arms.
- 1 Peter 5:4: Jesus is the Chief Shepherd who will reward those who faithfully serve Him.

PRAYER:

Dear Jesus, my Good Shepherd, thank You for loving me and laying down Your life for me. Thank You for guiding, protecting, and providing for me. Help me to trust You more each Day and to listen to Your voice. When I face difficulties, remind me of Your presence and Your care. May I find peace and rest, knowing that You are my Shepherd. Amen.

PERSONAL REFLECTION:

How does seeing Jesus as my Good Shepherd change my perspective on life's challenges? In what ways can I grow in trust and reliance on His guidance and care?

DAY 18: THE CRUCIFIXION: ATONEMENT FOR SIN

Scripture: Romans 5:8 (NASB)
"But God demonstrates His own love toward us, in that while we were yet sinners, Christ died for us."

ANECDOTE:

A man once owed a great debt he could never repay. He faced imprisonment and a life of hardship because of his inability to settle the debt. But then, a kind benefactor stepped in, offering to pay the entire debt on the man's behalf. This act of mercy not only freed the man from his financial burden but also gave him a new start in life.

APPLICATION:

The crucifixion of Jesus is the central event of the Christian faith. It is where God's love and justice meet. On the cross, Jesus took upon Himself the sins of the world, bearing the punishment that we deserved. Romans 5:8 powerfully reminds us that Christ died for us while we were still sinners. His sacrifice was not because we were deserving but because of His great love for us. Jesus' death on the cross was an act of atonement—He paid the debt of sin that we could never repay.

Understanding the crucifixion is essential for grasping the depth of God's love and the seriousness of sin. Sin separates us from God, and the wages of sin is death (Romans 6:23). But Jesus willingly endured the suffering and agony of the cross so that we could be reconciled to God. This act of love should lead us to repentance, gratitude, and worship. Knowing that Jesus paid the ultimate price for our forgiveness motivates us to live in a way that honors His sacrifice. The cross is a symbol of hope, reminding us that no matter how great our sin, God's grace is greater. Through faith in Jesus, we receive forgiveness, reconciliation, and the promise of eternal life.

FURTHER SCRIPTURE:

- 1 Peter 2:24: Jesus bore our sins in His body on the cross so that we might die to sin and live for righteousness.
- Isaiah 53:5: He was pierced for our transgressions and crushed for our iniquities.
- Colossians 2:13-14: God forgave our sins, canceling the charge of our legal indebtedness through the cross.

PRAYER:

Lord Jesus, thank You for dying on the cross for my sins. I am humbled and grateful for Your incredible love and sacrifice. Help me to never take for granted what You have done for me. May Your love transform my heart and lead me to live a life that reflects Your grace. Thank You for the hope and forgiveness that come through Your atoning sacrifice. Amen.

PERSONAL REFLECTION:

How does the crucifixion of Jesus impact my understanding of God's love and grace? What can I do to live in a way that honors His sacrifice for me?

DAY 19: THE RESURRECTION: VICTORY OVER DEATH

Scripture: 1 Corinthians 15:3-4 (NASB)
"For I delivered to you as of first importance what I also received, that Christ died for our sins according to the Scriptures, and that He was buried, and that He was raised on the third day according to the Scriptures."

ANECDOTE:

A story is told of a brave soldier who ventured into enemy territory to rescue his captured comrades. The odds were against him, and his mission seemed impossible. For Days, there was no word of his fate, and his friends feared the worst. But then, one morning he returned, victorious and unscathed, having defeated the enemy and set his comrades free. His return was not just a relief; it was a celebration of victory over what seemed like certain defeat.

APPLICATION:

The resurrection of Jesus is the cornerstone of the Christian faith. It is the definitive proof that Jesus is who He claimed to be—the Son of God and the Savior of the world. Paul emphasizes its importance in 1 Corinthians 15, stating that without the resurrection, our faith would be in vain. Jesus' resurrection is God's stamp of approval on His work of redemption, signifying that the power of sin and death has been defeated. By rising from the dead, Jesus demonstrated His victory over the grave and His authority over life and death.

The resurrection is not just a historical event; it has profound implications for our daily lives. Because Jesus lives, we, too, have the promise of eternal life. His resurrection gives us hope that death is not the end. For believers, death is a defeated enemy and eternal life is our inheritance. This truth should fill us with confidence and joy. It also empowers us to live boldly for Christ, knowing that the same power that raised Jesus from the dead is at work within us (Ephesians 1:19-20). The resurrection assures us that nothing—no hardship, trial, or persecution—can ultimately defeat us, for we are more than conquerors through Him who loved us (Romans 8:37).

FURTHER SCRIPTURE:

- John 11:25-26: Jesus declares that He is the resurrection and the life; whoever believes in Him will live, even though they die.
- Romans 6:4: We were buried with Christ through baptism into death, in order that we may live a new life through His resurrection.
- 1 Peter 1:3: Praise to God for a living hope through the resurrection of Jesus Christ from the dead.

PRAYER:

Risen Lord, thank You for Your victory over death. Thank You for the hope and assurance that come from knowing You are alive. Help me to live each Day in the power of Your resurrection, filled with hope and confidence. May my life be a testimony to Your life-giving power, and may I share the hope of the resurrection with others. Amen.

PERSONAL REFLECTION:

How does the resurrection of Jesus impact my daily life and my perspective on death? In what ways can I live more boldly, knowing that Jesus has conquered the grave?

DAY 20: JESUS, OUR MEDIATOR

Scripture: 1 Timothy 2:5 (NASB)
"For there is one God, and one mediator also be-
tween God and men, the man Christ Jesus."

ANECDOTE:

Consider a skilled lawyer who stands in court on behalf of a client. The client, facing severe accusations, relies entirely on the lawyer's expertise and advocacy. The lawyer speaks to the judge, presenting evidence, making appeals, and ensuring that justice is served and mercy is extended. Without the lawyer, the client would be lost; but with the lawyer, there is hope and a pathway to redemption.

APPLICATION:

Jesus as our Mediator is a comforting and powerful truth. A mediator is someone who stands between two parties to reconcile differences and bring about peace. We were separated from God because of our sin, and there was no way for us to bridge the gap on our own. Jesus, fully God and fully man, became the perfect Mediator who could reconcile us to God. He paid the penalty for our sins through His death on the cross, satisfying God's justice and demonstrating His love.

As our Mediator, Jesus continues to intercede for us before the Father. Hebrews 7:25 tells us that Jesus lives to make intercession for those who come to God through Him. This means that even now, Jesus is advocating on our behalf, ensuring that our relationship with God remains strong and secure. We can approach God with confidence, knowing that Jesus' mediation opens the way for us to receive mercy and grace. This assurance should fill us with peace and gratitude. It also reminds us that our relationship with God is not based on our efforts but on what Jesus has done and continues to do for us.

FURTHER SCRIPTURE:

- Hebrews 4:14-16: Jesus is our great high priest who sympathizes with our weaknesses and gives us confidence to approach the throne of grace.
- Romans 8:34: Jesus is at the right hand of God, interceding for us.
- Colossians 1:19-20: Through Jesus, God reconciled all things to Himself, making peace through His blood shed on the cross.

PRAYER:

Lord Jesus, thank You for being my Mediator and Advocate. Thank You for standing in the gap, reconciling me to God, and interceding on my behalf. Help me to rest in Your finished work, knowing that my relationship with God is secure because of You. May I live with confidence and gratitude, trusting in Your continual advocacy for me. Amen.

PERSONAL REFLECTION:

What does it mean for me to have Jesus as my Mediator? How does this truth change the way I approach God in prayer and in my daily life?

DAY 21: JESUS, THE COMING KING

Scripture: Revelation 19:11-16 (NASB)

"And I saw heaven opened, and behold, a white horse, and He who sat on it is called Faithful and True, and in righteousness He judges and wages war. His eyes are a flame of fire, and on His head are many diadems; and He has a name written on Him which no one knows except Himself. He is clothed with a robe dipped in blood, and His name is called The Word of God. And the armies which are in heaven, clothed in fine linen, white and clean, were following Him on white horses."

ANECDOTE:

A kingdom once faced a terrible threat from an invading army. The people were filled with fear and uncertainty, unsure if they would survive. Then, word came that their rightful king, long absent, was returning to reclaim his throne and defeat their enemies. Hope surged through the hearts of the people as they awaited the king's arrival. They knew that with their king leading the charge, victory was assured, and peace would be restored.

APPLICATION:

Jesus as the Coming King is a central hope of the Christian faith. Throughout the New Testament, believers are encouraged to live with the expectation that Jesus will return. In Revelation 19, John gives us a powerful vision of Jesus coming as a victorious king, riding on a white horse, and leading the armies of heaven. This imagery speaks of Jesus' authority, power, and righteousness. He comes to judge the nations, to bring justice, and to establish His kingdom in its fullness.

The promise of Jesus' return should inspire us to live with hope and purpose. It reminds us that this world, with all its suffering and injustice, is not our final home. Jesus will return to make all things new, to wipe away every tear, and to establish eternal peace. Knowing that Jesus is the coming King motivates us to live faithfully, to share the gospel, and to persevere through trials. It also encourages us to examine our hearts and lives, ensuring that we are ready for His return. Jesus' return is not just a future event: it shapes how we live today, as we seek to honor Him and live in light of His coming kingdom.

FURTHER SCRIPTURE:

- Matthew 24:30-31: The Son of Man will come on the clouds with power and great glory.
- Philippians 2:9-11: At the name of Jesus, every knee will bow, and every tongue confess that Jesus Christ is Lord.
- 1 Thessalonians 4:16-17: The Lord will descend from heaven, and believers will be caught up to meet Him.

PRAYER:

Lord Jesus, my Coming King, thank You for the promise of Your return. Thank You for the hope of a future where You reign in righteousness and peace. Help me to live each Day with expectation and readiness, seeking to honor You in all that I do. May my life be a reflection of Your kingdom, and may I share the hope of Your return with others. Amen.

PERSONAL REFLECTION:

How does the promise of Jesus' return impact my outlook on life and the world around me? What can I do toDay to live in a way that reflects my anticipation of His coming?

FIRMING UP YOUR FOUNDATION
JESUS CHRIST

- What does the incarnation of Jesus mean to you personally, and how does it influence your faith?

- Reflect on the sinless life of Christ. How does it set an example for your own life?

- How does viewing Jesus as the Good Shepherd bring comfort and guidance to you?

- In what ways has the crucifixion and resurrection of Jesus transformed your understanding of forgiveness and hope?

- What actions can you take to follow Jesus as King in your life?

WEEK 4
THE HOLY SPIRIT

DAY 22: THE HOLY SPIRIT IN SALVATION

Scripture: John 3:5-6 (NASB)

"Jesus answered, 'Truly, truly, I say to you, unless one is born of water and the Spirit he cannot enter into the kingdom of God. That which is born of the flesh is flesh, and that which is born of the Spirit is spirit.'"

ANECDOTE:

Imagine a person living in a dark room for many years, unaware that outside, a beautiful world filled with light and color awaits. One Day, someone opens a window and the room floods with light. The person's eyes adjust, and for the first time, they see the vibrant colors and the beauty outside. That light changes their entire perception of reality.

APPLICATION:

The Holy Spirit plays a vital role in the salvation of every believer. In John 3, Jesus tells Nicodemus that no one can enter the kingdom of God unless they are born of the Spirit. This new birth is not a physical rebirth but a spiritual one, where the Holy Spirit regenerates the heart, bringing a person from spiritual death to spiritual life. It's like moving from darkness into light. Without the Holy Spirit we remain spiritually dead, unable to see or understand the things of God.

The Holy Spirit's work in salvation involves convicting us of sin, revealing the truth of the gospel, and leading us to faith in Jesus Christ. It is the Holy Spirit who opens our eyes to see our need for a Savior and who enables us to respond in faith. This new birth transforms us from the inside out, making us new creations in Christ. Knowing that our salvation is the work of the Holy Spirit should fill us with gratitude and dependence. It's a reminder that our relationship with God is not based on our own efforts but on the Spirit's work in us. It also assures us that

God is actively at work in our lives, guiding and shaping us according to His purpose.

FURTHER SCRIPTURE:

- Titus 3:5: He saved us through the washing of rebirth and renewal by the Holy Spirit.
- 2 Corinthians 5:17: If anyone is in Christ, they are a new creation; the old has gone, the new has come.
- Romans 8:11: The Spirit who raised Jesus from the dead is living in us, giving life to our mortal bodies.

PRAYER:

Holy Spirit, thank You for bringing me to life in Christ. Thank You for convicting me of my sin and revealing my need for a Savior. Help me to rely on Your power and guidance each Day. May my life be a reflection of Your work in me, growing in faith and becoming more like Jesus. Amen.

PERSONAL REFLECTION:

How has the Holy Spirit worked in my life to bring me to faith in Jesus? In what ways can I be more aware and responsive to the Holy Spirit's leading each Day?

DAY 23: THE HOLY SPIRIT AS COMFORTER

Scripture: John 14:26 (NASB)
"But the Helper, the Holy Spirit, whom the Father will send in My name, He will teach you all things, and bring to your remembrance all that I said to you."

ANECDOTE:

A child feels lost and frightened in a crowded place, separated from its parent. Just as fear begins to overwhelm the child, it feels a familiar hand gently take hold. Turning, it sees its parent's reassuring face. The fear melts away, replaced by a sense of safety and comfort. The child knows that as long as its parent is near, everything will be okay.

APPLICATION:

Jesus referred to the Holy Spirit as the "Helper" or "Comforter," emphasizing the Spirit's role in providing support, guidance, and reassurance to believers. In John 14 Jesus promised He would send the Holy Spirit to be with His disciples after He returned to the Father. The Holy Spirit's presence would continue Jesus' work, teaching, guiding, and comforting them. This promise is for all believers. The Holy Spirit dwells within us, providing comfort in times of fear, uncertainty, and sorrow.

The Holy Spirit's comfort is not just about making us feel better, it's about reminding us of God's truth and presence. The Spirit brings to our remembrance the words of Jesus, assuring us of His promises and love. In moments of anxiety or grief the Holy Spirit is the one who whispers peace to our hearts, reminding us that God is with us and for us. This comfort gives us strength to endure trials and courage to face the unknown. Knowing that the Holy Spirit is our Comforter should lead us to seek His presence in prayer, to listen for His voice in God's Word, and to rely on His guidance in our daily lives.

FURTHER SCRIPTURE:

- Romans 8:26: The Spirit helps us in our weakness and intercedes for us.
- Psalm 34:18: The Lord is near to the brokenhearted and saves the crushed in spirit.
- 2 Corinthians 1:3-4: God is the God of all comfort, who comforts us in all our troubles.

PRAYER:

Holy Spirit, my Comforter, thank You for Your presence in my life. Thank You for bringing peace to my heart when I am anxious and for reminding me of God's truth when I am uncertain. Help me to turn to You in every situation, trusting in Your guidance and comfort. May I find strength and hope in Your presence each Day. Amen.

PERSONAL REFLECTION:

When have I experienced the Holy Spirit's comfort in my life? How can I lean more on the Holy Spirit for guidance and peace during difficult times?

DAY 24: THE INDWELLING SPIRIT

Scripture: 1 Corinthians 6:19-20 (NASB)
*"Or do you not know that your body is a temple of the
Holy Spirit who is in you, whom you have from God,
and that you are not your own? For you have been bought
with a price: therefore glorify God in your body."*

ANECDOTE:

A king decided to dwell among his people, not in a grand palace far removed from daily life, but in a simple house in the midst of the city. His presence brought peace, justice, and prosperity to the land. Knowing that their king lived among them, the people lived with a sense of honor and purpose, aware that they were always in his presence.

APPLICATION:

One of the most profound truths of the Christian faith is that the Holy Spirit dwells within believers. Paul reminds the Corinthians that their bodies are temples of the Holy Spirit, emphasizing the intimate and personal relationship we have with God. The Holy Spirit's indwelling presence means that God is not distant; He is near, actively involved in our daily lives. This reality changes everything. Knowing that the Holy Spirit lives within us should lead to a deep sense of awe and responsibility.

The indwelling Spirit empowers us to live holy lives, guiding us in truth, convicting us of sin, and enabling us to serve God effectively. It is the Holy Spirit who gives us the strength to overcome temptation, the wisdom to make godly decisions, and the courage to witness for Christ. Our bodies, as temples of the Holy Spirit, are to be treated with respect, honoring God in how we live, speak, and think. This truth reminds us that we belong to God, purchased by the blood of Jesus, and our lives are to reflect His glory.

FURTHER SCRIPTURE:

- Romans 8:9-11: The Spirit of God lives in us, and we belong to Him.
- Galatians 2:20: It is no longer we who live, but Christ lives in us.
- Ezekiel 36:27: God's promise to put His Spirit within us and move us to follow His decrees.

PRAYER:

Holy Spirit, thank You for dwelling within me. Thank You for being my constant companion, guide, and strength. Help me to live in a way that honors You, recognizing that my body is Your temple. May my thoughts, words, and actions reflect Your presence in my life. Empower me to serve and glorify God each Day. Amen.

PERSONAL REFLECTION:

How does knowing that the Holy Spirit lives within me change my view of myself and my daily life? In what ways can I honor the Holy Spirit's presence in my body and actions?

DAY 25: THE FRUITS OF THE SPIRIT

Scripture: Galatians 5:22-23 (NASB)
*"But the fruit of the Spirit is love, joy, peace, pa-
tience, kindness, goodness, faithfulness, gentleness,
self-control; against such things there is no law."*

ANECDOTE:

A gardener carefully tends to his orchard, watering the trees, pruning branches, and ensuring they have the right nutrients. Over time, the trees produce abundant fruit not by their own effort, but because of the care and attention of the gardener. The fruit reflects the health of the tree and the skill of the gardener.

APPLICATION:

The fruit of the Spirit are the natural result of the Holy Spirit's work in our lives. Just as healthy trees bear good fruit, a life surrendered to the Holy Spirit will exhibit these characteristics: love, joy, peace, patience, kindness, goodness, faithfulness, gentleness, and self-control. They are not produced by our own efforts; they are the evidence of God's Spirit actively working in us. As we remain connected to God through prayer, scripture, and obedience, the Holy Spirit cultivates these qualities within us.

These fruits stand in contrast to the works of the flesh—such as anger, jealousy, and selfishness—that arise from our sinful nature. The Holy Spirit's presence in our lives empowers us to overcome our natural tendencies and to reflect Christ's character. The fruits of the Spirit also impact our relationships, making us more loving, patient, and kind toward others. When people see these qualities in us, they see a glimpse of God's character and are drawn to Him. Growing in the fruit of the Spirit is a lifelong process, but it begins with daily surrender to God's will and sensitivity to the Spirit's leading.

FURTHER SCRIPTURE:

- John 15:4-5: Abiding in Christ leads to bearing much fruit.
- Matthew 7:17-20: A good tree produces good fruit.
- Ephesians 5:9: The fruit of the light consists in all goodness, righteousness, and truth.

PRAYER:

Holy Spirit, help me to bear the fruit of Your presence in my life. Cultivate love, joy, peace, patience, kindness, goodness, faithfulness, gentleness, and self-control in me. I surrender my will to You, and I ask that You transform my heart to reflect the character of Christ. May my life be a testimony to Your power and grace. Amen.

PERSONAL REFLECTION:

Which fruits of the Spirit do I see growing in my life? In what areas do I need to ask the Holy Spirit for more growth and transformation?

DAY 26: BEING FILLED WITH THE SPIRIT

Scripture: Ephesians 5:18 (NASB)
"And do not get drunk with wine, for that is dissipation, but be filled with the Spirit."

ANECDOTE:

Imagine a sailboat out on the ocean. For the boat to move forward, it needs the wind to fill its sails. Without the wind, the boat is at the mercy of the waves, drifting aimlessly. But when the wind blows, the sails fill, and the boat moves with purpose and direction, guided by the skilled hand of its captain.

APPLICATION:

Paul's instruction to be filled with the Spirit is a call to live under the influence and guidance of the Holy Spirit, much like a sailboat is moved by the wind. Being filled with the Spirit is not a one-time event but a continuous, daily surrender to God's will. It involves yielding our desires, thoughts, and actions to the control of the Holy Spirit. Just as a person under the influence of alcohol may act differently, a person filled with the Spirit will display Christ-like behavior and attitudes.

The filling of the Spirit leads to a life characterized by joy, worship, thankfulness, and mutual submission. It empowers us for service, equips us for ministry, and enables us to resist temptation. Being filled with the Spirit means allowing Him to influence every area of our lives, making us more like Jesus. To be filled with the Spirit, we need to seek God in prayer, immerse ourselves in His Word, and be sensitive to His leading. It requires humility and a willingness to be changed from the inside out.

FURTHER SCRIPTURE:

- Acts 4:31: Believers were filled with the Holy Spirit and spoke the word of God boldly.
- Galatians 5:16: Walking by the Spirit prevents us from carrying out the desires of the flesh.
- Colossians 3:16: Letting the word of Christ dwell in us richly leads to Spirit-filled living.

PRAYER:

Holy Spirit, fill me with Your presence toDay. I surrender my will and my life to Your control. Guide my thoughts, words, and actions so that they reflect Your love and truth. Empower me to serve others and to walk in a way that honors God. May my life be a vessel through which Your Spirit flows. Amen.

PERSONAL REFLECTION:

What does it mean for me to be filled with the Holy Spirit? How can I create space in my life for the Holy Spirit to fill and guide me each Day?

DAY 27: THE GIFTS OF THE SPIRIT

Scripture: 1 Corinthians 12:4-6 (NASB)
"Now there are varieties of gifts, but the same Spirit. And there are varieties of ministries, and the same Lord. There are varieties of effects, but the same God who works all things in all persons."

ANECDOTE:

A symphony orchestra is made up of different instruments, each with its unique sound and role. The strings, woodwinds, brass, and percussion all contribute to the beauty of the music. When each musician plays their part the result is a harmonious and powerful performance that moves and inspires those who listen.

APPLICATION:

The Holy Spirit gives spiritual gifts to every believer for the purpose of building up the body of Christ and serving others. These gifts are diverse, ranging from teaching, healing, prophecy, and administration to acts of mercy and encouragement. Just as a symphony requires different instruments to create beautiful music, the church requires a variety of gifts to function effectively and to reflect God's glory. The gifts of the Spirit are not given for personal pride or gain but for the common good.

Understanding that each believer has a gift from the Spirit encourages us to value and appreciate the unique contributions of others. It also challenges us to use our gifts faithfully, seeking to serve rather than be served. We may not all have the same gifts, but each gift is important in God's plan. As we serve in the areas where the Holy Spirit has gifted us, we experience joy and fulfillment, and the church is strengthened. Discovering and using our spiritual gifts involves prayer, seeking God's guidance, and being willing to step out in faith.

FURTHER SCRIPTURE:

- Romans 12:6-8: Different gifts according to the grace given to each of us.
- Ephesians 4:11-12: Christ gave different ministry gifts to equip His people for works of service.
- 1 Peter 4:10: Each one should use whatever gift they have received to serve others.

PRAYER:

Holy Spirit, thank You for the gifts You have given to me and to others in the body of Christ. Help me to recognize and use my gifts to serve You and to build up Your church. May I be a faithful steward of the gifts You have entrusted to me, and may I encourage others in their gifts as well. Let our collective efforts bring glory to God. Amen.

PERSONAL REFLECTION:

What spiritual gifts do I believe the Holy Spirit has given me? How can I use these gifts to serve others and build up the church?

DAY 28: WALKING IN THE SPIRIT

Scripture: Galatians 5:16 (NASB)
*"But I say, walk by the Spirit, and you will
not carry out the desire of the flesh."*

ANECDOTE:

A traveler sets out on a journey through a dense forest. The path is not clear, and there are many forks and obstacles along the way. However, the traveler has a guide who knows the forest intimately. By following the guide closely the traveler avoids dangers, finds the right path, and reaches the destination safely. The journey is successful because of the guidance provided.

APPLICATION:

Walking in the Spirit means living our daily lives under the guidance and influence of the Holy Spirit. It is a continual process of yielding to the Spirit's leading rather than following our own desires or the ways of the world. Paul's exhortation in Galatians 5:16 highlights the conflict between the flesh and the Spirit. The flesh represents our sinful nature, which leads us away from God. The Spirit leads us toward righteousness, peace, and life. To walk in the Spirit, we must be intentional about seeking God's will and submitting to His direction.

This walk involves prayer, reading Scripture, and being sensitive to the Spirit's promptings. It requires us to be aware of our thoughts, attitudes, and actions, choosing to align them with God's Word. When we walk in the Spirit, we experience the fruits of the Spirit in our lives and gain victory over sin. It is not about perfection but about progression—growing closer to God each day and allowing His Spirit to transform us. Walking in the Spirit brings freedom, joy, and fulfillment, as we live out God's purpose for our lives.

FURTHER SCRIPTURE:

- Romans 8:4: We are called to walk according to the Spirit and not according to the flesh.
- Ephesians 5:8-10: Walk as children of light, trying to discern what is pleasing to the Lord.
- John 16:13: The Spirit of truth guides us into all truth.

PRAYER:

Holy Spirit, help me to walk with You each Day. Guide my steps, direct my thoughts, and lead my actions so that I may honor God. Give me the strength to resist the desires of the flesh and to choose what is right and good. May my life reflect the light of Your presence, and may I grow closer to You with each passing Day. Amen.

PERSONAL REFLECTION:

What does it look like for me to walk in the Spirit in my daily life? How can I be more aware of the Holy Spirit's guidance and seek to follow His lead.

FIRMING UP YOUR FAITH
THE HOLY SPIRIT

- How has learning about the role of the Holy Spirit in salvation strengthened your faith?

- What new understanding did you gain about the Holy Spirit as Comforter and Guide?

- Reflect on the gifts and fruits of the Spirit. How can you cultivate these in your life?

- What steps can you take to be more aware of and filled with the Spirit daily?

- How can you walk more closely with the Spirit and depend on His guidance?

WEEK 5
THE BIBLE

DAY 29: THE INSPIRATION OF SCRIPTURE

DAY 30: THE AUTHORITY
OF GOD'S WORD

DAY 31: THE BIBLE AS OUR GUIDE

DAY 32: UNDERSTANDING GOD'S WORD

DAY 33: MEDITATING ON SCRIPTURE

DAY 34: APPLYING THE WORD
TO OUR LIVES

DAY 35: THE ROLE OF THE HOLY
SPIRIT IN BIBLE STUDY

DAY 29: THE INSPIRATION OF SCRIPTURE

Scripture: 2 Timothy 3:16-17 (NASB)

"All Scripture is inspired by God and profitable for teaching, for reproof, for correction, for training in righteousness; so that the man of God may be adequate, equipped for every good work."

ANECDOTE:

A young apprentice once sought wisdom from a master craftsman. The master handed him a well-worn book and said, "In these pages, you will find the guidance and knowledge you need to excel. This book has been passed down from generation to generation, and its principles are timeless." The apprentice found that whenever he faced a challenge, the answers were there in the master's book, guiding him toward excellence.

APPLICATION:

The Bible is not just a collection of ancient writings; it is the inspired Word of God. The term "inspired" means "God-breathed," indicating that Scripture is directly from God. While human authors penned the words they did so under the guidance and influence of the Holy Spirit. This divine inspiration means that the Bible is trustworthy and authoritative. It reveals God's character, His will, and His plan for humanity.

Paul's words to Timothy emphasize that Scripture is profitable for teaching, reproof, correction, and training in righteousness. It equips us for every good work, helping us to grow in faith and live according to God's standards. Recognizing the inspiration of Scripture should lead us to approach the Bible with reverence, humility, and a desire to learn. It is a living document that speaks to us today, offering wisdom, guidance, and the truth we need to navigate life's challenges.

FURTHER SCRIPTURE:

- 2 Peter 1:20-21: Prophecy in Scripture came from men moved by the Holy Spirit, not from human will.
- Psalm 119:105: God's Word is a lamp to our feet and a light to our path.
- Hebrews 4:12: The Word of God is living, active, and sharper than any two-edged sword.

PRAYER:

Heavenly Father, thank You for the gift of Your Word. Thank You for speaking to us through the Scriptures, revealing Your truth and guiding our lives. Help me to approach the Bible with reverence and openness, ready to learn and be transformed. May Your Word equip me for every good work and draw me closer to You. Amen.

PERSONAL REFLECTION:

How do I view the Bible in my daily life? In what ways can I deepen my commitment to reading and applying God's inspired Word?

DAY 30: THE AUTHORITY OF GOD'S WORD

Scripture: Isaiah 40:8 (NASB)
"The grass withers, the flower fades, but the word of our God stands forever."

ANECDOTE:

In a courtroom, the judge's words carry authority. Everyone listens when the judge speaks, knowing that his decisions can change lives and uphold justice. His authority is respected because it is backed by the law. Similarly, the Bible holds authority in the life of a believer because it is backed by the ultimate authority—God Himself.

APPLICATION:

The authority of the Bible means that it is the final word on all matters of faith and practice. Unlike human opinions or cultural trends that change with time, God's Word stands forever. It is unchanging, reliable, and true. Isaiah 40:8 reminds us that while everything else in life may fade away, God's Word remains. This enduring authority is rooted in the fact that Scripture is God-breathed, making it a trustworthy guide for our lives.

When we recognize the authority of the Bible, it shapes how we live, make decisions, and understand the world around us. We submit to God's Word, even when it challenges us or goes against popular opinion. The Bible becomes our standard for truth, guiding us in what to believe and how to act. Submitting to its authority means allowing it to correct us, instruct us, and lead us into righteousness. By embracing the Bible's authority, we find stability and direction in an ever-changing world.

FURTHER SCRIPTURE:

- Matthew 24:35: Jesus said heaven and earth will pass away, but His words will never pass away.
- Psalm 119:89: God's Word is firmly fixed in the heavens.
- Proverbs 30:5-6: Every word of God is flawless; He is a shield to those who take refuge in Him.

PRAYER:

Lord, I acknowledge the authority of Your Word over my life. Help me to submit to its teachings and to trust in its truth. Give me the humility to accept correction and the courage to live according to Your will. May Your Word be my foundation and guide in all that I do. Amen.

PERSONAL REFLECTION:

Do I view the Bible as the ultimate authority in my life? How can I align my actions and beliefs more closely with God's Word?

DAY 31: THE BIBLE AS OUR GUIDE

Scripture: Psalm 119:105 (NASB)
"Your word is a lamp to my feet and a light to my path."

ANECDOTE:

A traveler in the desert found himself caught in a sudden storm, with darkness falling quickly. Without a light he would lose his way and be in danger. Thankfully, he had a lantern in his pack. By lighting the lantern, he could see the path ahead, step by step, safely making his way through the storm and finding shelter.

APPLICATION:

Life is full of uncertainty and challenges, much like navigating through a dark and stormy night. In such times, we need a reliable guide to show us the way. Psalm 119:105 beautifully describes God's Word as a lamp and a light that guides our steps. The Bible provides wisdom, direction, and clarity, helping us make decisions that align with God's will. It reveals the right path, leading us away from danger and toward safety.

God's Word does not necessarily show us the entire journey at once; often, it illuminates just the next step. This teaches us to walk by faith, trusting God's guidance one day at a time. By immersing ourselves in Scripture, we gain discernment to recognize God's voice and follow His leading. The Bible equips us to face moral dilemmas, relational conflicts, and life's uncertainties with confidence and grace. As we rely on God's Word, we find a steady and sure guide, one that never fails us.

FURTHER SCRIPTURE:

- Proverbs 3:5-6: Trust in the Lord with all your heart, and He will make your paths straight.
- Joshua 1:8: Meditate on the Book of the Law day and night for success and prosperity.
- James 1:5: If we lack wisdom we should ask God, who gives generously.

PRAYER:

Lord, thank You for Your Word, which guides me in all areas of life. Help me to seek Your guidance in Scripture daily, trusting in Your wisdom and direction. When I face uncertainty, let Your Word be my light, showing me the next step to take. May I walk in the path of Your truth and find peace and safety in Your presence. Amen.

PERSONAL REFLECTION:

In what areas of my life do I need God's guidance the most right now? How can I use Scripture to find clarity and direction in those areas?

DAY 32: UNDERSTANDING GOD'S WORD

Scripture: James 1:22 (NASB)
"But prove yourselves doers of the word, and not merely hearers who delude themselves."

ANECDOTE:

A student received a detailed manual for operating a complex machine. He read the manual carefully but never actually put what he learned into practice. When it came time to use the machine, he realized that knowledge alone wasn't enough; he needed experience and application to truly understand how to operate it.

APPLICATION:

Hearing God's Word is important, but understanding it comes through doing—through living it out in our daily lives. James warns against merely listening to the Word and not acting on it, likening such a person to someone who looks at their reflection in a mirror and immediately forgets what they look like. Understanding God's Word involves more than intellectual knowledge, it requires application. When we apply Scripture to our lives, it transforms us, shaping our character and actions.

Applying God's Word means putting its principles into practice, whether it's showing love to others, forgiving those who wrong us, or living with integrity and honesty. It means letting Scripture guide our decisions, influence our behavior, and mold our relationships. Understanding God's Word also involves prayer and reliance on the Holy Spirit. We ask for insight and wisdom, knowing that the Spirit helps us grasp the deeper meanings of Scripture and how it applies to our specific situations. True understanding of God's Word leads to a changed life, reflecting the image of Christ more and more each day.

FURTHER SCRIPTURE:

- Psalm 119:18: "Open my eyes, that I may behold wonderful things from Your law."
- Luke 11:28: Blessed are those who hear the word of God and keep it.
- 2 Timothy 2:15: Be diligent to present yourself approved to God, accurately handling the word of truth.

PRAYER:

Lord, help me not only to hear Your Word but to understand and apply it in my life. Give me the wisdom to see how Your teachings apply to my daily circumstances. May Your Word take root in my heart and bear fruit in my actions. Let my life reflect Your truth, and may others see You in me. Amen.

PERSONAL REFLECTION:

How can I be more intentional about applying God's Word to my daily life? What steps can I take to become a doer of the Word and not just a hearer?

DAY 33: MEDITATING ON SCRIPTURE

Scripture: Psalm 1:2 (NASB)
"But his delight is in the law of the Lord, and in His law he meditates day and night."

ANECDOTE:

A musician practices his instrument every Day, not just playing the notes but truly internalizing the music. He listens intently, repeats difficult sections, and feels the emotion behind the melody. Through consistent practice and reflection the music becomes a part of him, allowing him to perform with passion and confidence.

APPLICATION:

Meditating on Scripture is like internalizing a piece of music. It's more than just reading; it's reflecting deeply, pondering its meaning, and allowing it to permeate our thoughts and hearts. Psalm 1 describes the blessed person as one who delights in God's law and meditates on it Day and night. This continuous meditation transforms our thinking, aligns our desires with God's, and strengthens our faith.

Meditation on Scripture helps us to understand God's will, hear His voice more clearly, and apply His Word to our lives. It's like letting the seeds of God's truth sink deeply into the soil of our hearts, where they can grow and bear fruit. Meditating on Scripture can take many forms: memorizing verses, reflecting on a passage, or prayerfully considering its application. The key is to make it a regular practice, turning our minds to God's Word throughout the day. As we meditate on Scripture, we experience God's peace, wisdom, and guidance more fully.

FURTHER SCRIPTURE:

- Joshua 1:8: Meditate on the Book of the Law day and night for success.
- Colossians 3:16: Let the word of Christ dwell in you richly.
- Psalm 119:97: "Oh, how I love Your law! It is my meditation all the day."

PRAYER:

Lord, help me to delight in Your Word and to meditate on it Day and night. Teach me to reflect deeply on Your truth, letting it shape my thoughts, desires, and actions. May Your Word be a source of joy and strength in my life, guiding me in all that I do. Draw me closer to You as I meditate on Your Scriptures. Amen.

PERSONAL REFLECTION:

How can I make meditation on God's Word a regular part of my daily routine? What benefits have I experienced when I take time to reflect deeply on Scripture?

DAY 34: APPLYING THE WORD TO OUR LIVES

Scripture: Matthew 7:24 (NASB)
*"Therefore everyone who hears these words of Mine
and acts on them, may be compared to a wise
man who built his house on the rock."*

ANECDOTE:

A builder carefully follows the architect's blueprints, making sure every measurement and material is precisely as specified. By adhering to the plan, the builder ensures that the structure is strong, stable, and able to withstand storms. Without following the blueprint, the house would be at risk of collapse.

APPLICATION:

Jesus' parable of the wise and foolish builders illustrates the importance of applying God's Word to our lives. Hearing God's Word is like receiving a blueprint for life. But just hearing it is not enough; we must act on it. The wise builder hears Jesus' words and puts them into practice, building a life on a solid foundation. The foolish builder hears but does not act, building on a shaky foundation that cannot withstand life's storms.

Applying God's Word means living out its principles daily. It involves making choices that reflect God's character, loving others, forgiving, seeking justice, and walking in humility. It means allowing Scripture to influence our decisions, our relationships, and our view of the world. Building on the rock of God's Word provides stability, security, and peace, even in difficult times. By committing to apply the Bible's teachings, we build a life that honors God and withstands the challenges we face.

FURTHER SCRIPTURE:

- James 1:25: The one who looks intently at the perfect law and abides by it will be blessed.
- Luke 11:28: Blessed are those who hear the word of God and keep it.
- Proverbs 3:1-2: Keep God's commandments, for they bring peace and prosperity.

PRAYER:

Lord, thank You for Your Word, which is a firm foundation for my life. Help me to be a wise builder, not only hearing Your words but putting them into practice. Show me how to apply Your teachings in my daily life, and give me the strength to follow through. May my life be a reflection of Your truth, built on the solid rock of Your Word. Amen.

PERSONAL REFLECTION:

In what areas of my life do I need to more actively apply God's Word? How can I be intentional about living out the principles of Scripture each Day?

DAY 35: THE ROLE OF THE HOLY SPIRIT IN BIBLE STUDY

Scripture: John 16:13 (NASB)
*"But when He, the Spirit of truth, comes, He will guide
you into all the truth; for He will not speak on His
own initiative, but whatever He hears, He will speak;
and He will disclose to you what is to come."*

ANECDOTE:

A traveler is given a map to navigate a foreign land. The map is detailed and accurate, but without a guide who understands the terrain, it's difficult to make sense of the directions. With the guide's help, the traveler can interpret the map correctly and find the best paths, avoiding dangers and reaching the destination safely.

APPLICATION:

The Holy Spirit plays a crucial role in understanding and applying the Bible. Jesus called the Holy Spirit the "Spirit of truth" who would guide believers into all truth. When we study the Bible, we rely on the Holy Spirit to open our eyes, help us understand God's Word, and apply it to our lives. The Holy Spirit illuminates Scripture, revealing its deeper meanings and showing us how it applies to our specific situations.

Studying the Bible without the guidance of the Holy Spirit is like trying to read a map without understanding the terrain. The Spirit helps us discern God's voice, convicts us of sin, and leads us into wisdom and righteousness. Before reading Scripture, it's important to pray, asking the Holy Spirit for insight, understanding, and a receptive heart. As we yield to the Spirit's leading, we grow in knowledge, faith, and obedience, becoming more aligned with God's will.

FURTHER SCRIPTURE:

- 1 Corinthians 2:10-12: The Spirit reveals God's deep things, giving us understanding.
- Psalm 119:18: "Open my eyes, that I may behold wonderful things from Your law."
- Ephesians 1:17: Paul prays for the Spirit of wisdom and revelation to know God better.

PRAYER:

Holy Spirit, thank You for being my guide as I study God's Word. Open my eyes to see the truth and give me understanding to apply it to my life. Lead me into all truth, convict me where I need to change, and strengthen me to follow God's will. May my time in Scripture draw me closer to You and transform my heart. Amen.

PERSONAL REFLECTION:

How have I experienced the Holy Spirit's guidance in my Bible study? What can I do to rely more on the Spirit's insight and understanding as I read Scripture?

FIRMING UP YOUR FAITH
THE BIBLE

- How does understanding the inspiration of Scripture affect your approach to reading the Bible?

- What steps can you take to apply the authority of God's Word in your daily life?

- In what ways has the Bible served as a guide for you this week?

- How can you meditate on Scripture more deeply and apply it practically?

- How does the Holy Spirit help you in studying and understanding the Bible?

WEEK 6
PRAYER

DAY 36: THE IMPORTANCE OF PRAYER

Scripture: Philippians 4:6-7 (NASB)

"Be anxious for nothing, but in everything by prayer and supplication with thanksgiving let your requests be made known to God. And the peace of God, which surpasses all comprehension, will guard your hearts and your minds in Christ Jesus."

ANECDOTE:

A young child falls and scrapes her knee. Instinctively, she runs to her mother, seeking comfort and care. Her mother soothes her, cleans the wound, and reassures her that everything will be okay. The child's fear melts away, replaced by the peace and security of being in her mother's arms.

APPLICATION:

Prayer is a powerful and essential part of the Christian life. It is our way of communicating with God, bringing our needs, fears, and desires before Him. In Philippians 4:6-7, Paul encourages believers to bring everything to God in prayer, rather than being anxious. Prayer is an invitation to experience God's peace, even in the midst of difficult circumstances. It's not just about presenting requests; it's about building a relationship with God, trusting Him with our deepest concerns, and allowing His presence to calm our hearts.

Prayer shifts our focus from our problems to God's power. When we pray, we acknowledge that God is in control, and we are not alone. Prayer also invites God's guidance and wisdom into our lives, helping us make decisions that honor Him. Through prayer, we find strength, comfort, and direction. It's a reminder that we have a loving Father who cares for us and listens to us. Making prayer a daily habit helps us stay connected to God, grow in faith, and experience His peace that surpasses all understanding.

FURTHER SCRIPTURE:

- 1 Thessalonians 5:17: Pray without ceasing.
- Matthew 6:6: Jesus teaches us to pray in secret, where God hears us.
- Jeremiah 29:12: God promises to listen when we call upon Him in prayer.

PRAYER:

Heavenly Father, thank You for the privilege of prayer. Help me to bring all my concerns and needs to You, trusting that You hear and care for me. May Your peace fill my heart and mind, guarding me against anxiety. Draw me closer to You through prayer, and let my life be a reflection of Your love and grace. Amen.

PERSONAL REFLECTION:

How can I make prayer a more consistent part of my daily routine? What specific concerns do I need to bring before God in prayer toDay?

DAY 37: THE LORD'S PRAYER AS A MODEL

Scripture: Matthew 6:9-13 (NASB)

"Pray, then, in this way: 'Our Father who is in heaven, Hallowed be Your name. Your kingdom come. Your will be done, On earth as it is in heaven. Give us this day our daily bread. And forgive us our debts, as we also have forgiven our debtors. And do not lead us into temptation, but deliver us from evil.'"

ANECDOTE:

A group of athletes looks to their coach for direction before a big game. The coach outlines the strategy, emphasizing the importance of teamwork, discipline, and focus. The team knows that by following their coach's plan, they have the best chance of success. They trust his experience and wisdom to guide them.

APPLICATION:

The Lord's Prayer, taught by Jesus in the Sermon on the Mount, serves as a model for how we should pray. It begins with recognizing God's holiness and our relationship with Him as our Father. This opening sets the tone for reverence, trust, and intimacy. The prayer then expresses a desire for God's kingdom to come and His will to be done, reminding us to align our desires with God's purposes.

By asking for daily bread, we acknowledge our dependence on God for our needs. Seeking forgiveness and offering forgiveness highlights the importance of grace in our relationships. Finally, asking for deliverance from temptation and evil acknowledges our need for God's protection and guidance. The Lord's Prayer covers every aspect of life: God's glory, our needs, relationships, and spiritual well-being. Using it as a model helps us develop a balanced and comprehensive prayer life. It reminds us to focus on God's character and kingdom, seek His provision, live in forgiveness, and rely on His strength.

FURTHER SCRIPTURE:

- Luke 11:1: The disciples ask Jesus to teach them to pray.
- Psalm 103:13: As a father has compassion on his children, so the Lord has compassion on those who fear Him.
- 1 John 1:9: If we confess our sins, God is faithful to forgive us.

PRAYER:

Our Father in heaven, hallowed be Your name. Your kingdom come, Your will be done, on earth as it is in heaven. Give us toDay our daily bread. Forgive us our debts, as we forgive our debtors. Lead us not into temptation, but deliver us from evil. For Yours is the kingdom and the power and the glory forever. Amen.

PERSONAL REFLECTION:

How can I use the Lord's Prayer as a guide in my daily prayer life? What areas of my life do I need to surrender to God's will toDay?

DAY 38: PRAYING IN FAITH

Scripture: Mark 11:24 (NASB)
"Therefore I say to you, all things for which you pray and ask, believe that you have received them, and they will be granted you."

ANECDOTE:

A farmer plants seeds in his field, even though he cannot see what lies beneath the soil. He waters the seeds, tends the field, and waits patiently, trusting that in time, the seeds will sprout and grow into a bountiful harvest. His faith in the process keeps him diligent and hopeful, knowing that his efforts will bear fruit.

APPLICATION:

Praying in faith means approaching God with confidence, believing that He hears and will answer according to His will. Jesus' words in Mark 11:24 encourage us to believe that we have received what we ask for in prayer. This kind of faith is not about demanding things from God but trusting in His power, wisdom, and goodness. Faith in prayer acknowledges that God knows what is best for us and will answer in His perfect timing.

Praying in faith requires us to align our desires with God's will, seeking His purposes above our own. It means trusting that God is able to do far more than we can ask or imagine (Ephesians 3:20). When we pray with faith, we release our worries and fears, knowing that God is in control. This trust leads to peace, even when we don't see immediate answers. Faith-filled prayer also involves persistence, continuing to seek God's presence and guidance, confident that He is at work. By praying in faith, we deepen our relationship with God and experience His power and love in new ways.

FURTHER SCRIPTURE:

- James 1:6: When asking in prayer, we must believe and not doubt.
- Hebrews 11:6: Without faith, it is impossible to please God.
- Matthew 21:22: Whatever we ask in prayer, believing, we will receive.

PRAYER:

Lord, I come to You in faith, believing that You hear my prayers and that You know what is best for me. Help me to trust in Your power and wisdom, even when I don't understand. Increase my faith and give me the courage to pray boldly, seeking Your will in all things. Thank You for Your faithfulness and love. Amen.

PERSONAL REFLECTION:

How does my level of faith influence my prayer life? What steps can I take to grow in faith and trust when I pray?

DAY 39: PERSISTENCE IN PRAYER

Scripture: Luke 18:1 (NASB)
*"Now He was telling them a parable to show that at
all times they ought to pray and not to lose heart."*

ANECDOTE:

A child repeatedly asks her father for a new toy, showing her desire and persistence. The father, observing his daughter's genuine interest, waits before responding to see if the desire is fleeting or sincere. Over time, as the child continues to ask, the father recognizes her commitment and grants her request, not just to please her but to teach her the value of persistence and patience.

APPLICATION:

Persistence in prayer is a powerful demonstration of faith and dependence on God. Jesus' parable in Luke 18 about the persistent widow illustrates the importance of praying without giving up. The widow's constant requests moved the unjust judge to action; how much more will our loving Heavenly Father respond to His children's persistent prayers? Persistence in prayer is not about convincing God to act but about showing our faith and trust in Him.

Persistent prayer deepens our relationship with God, keeping us focused on His presence and purpose. It teaches us patience, dependence, and perseverance. When we pray persistently, we learn to align our will with God's, seeking His kingdom above our own desires. Even when answers are delayed, persistent prayer reminds us that God is at work, often in ways we cannot see. It encourages us to keep knocking, trusting that God's timing is perfect and His answers are always for our good.

FURTHER SCRIPTURE:

- 1 Thessalonians 5:17: Pray without ceasing.
- Colossians 4:2: Devote yourselves to prayer, being watchful and thankful.
- Matthew 7:7: Ask, and it will be given to you; seek, and you will find; knock, and it will be opened to you.

PRAYER:

Heavenly Father, teach me to be persistent in prayer, trusting that You hear and respond in Your perfect timing. Help me not to lose heart when answers are delayed but to continue seeking Your presence and guidance. Strengthen my faith, and may my persistence reflect my trust in Your goodness and love. Amen.

PERSONAL REFLECTION:

Are there specific areas in my life where I need to be more persistent in prayer? How can I develop a habit of persistent prayer, even when I don't see immediate results?

DAY 40: INTERCESSORY PRAYER

Scripture: 1 Timothy 2:1 (NASB)

> *"First of all, then, I urge that entreaties and prayers, petitions and thanksgivings, be made on behalf of all men."*

ANECDOTE:

A soldier on the battlefield radios back to his base, requesting support and assistance for his comrades. Though he is not alone in the fight, he knows that additional support can turn the tide of battle. His call for help reflects his concern for others and his trust in the support system that backs him.

APPLICATION:

Intercessory prayer is the act of praying on behalf of others, lifting their needs and concerns to God. Paul encourages Timothy to make prayers and petitions for all people, highlighting the importance of intercession in the Christian life. Through intercessory prayer, we participate in God's work, standing in the gap for others and seeking God's intervention in their lives.

Intercession shows love, compassion, and a sense of responsibility for our brothers and sisters in Christ. It acknowledges our interconnectedness as members of the body of Christ. When we intercede for others, we bring their struggles, hopes, and fears before God, trusting Him to work in their lives. Intercessory prayer is an expression of faith, as we believe that God is able to provide healing, guidance, and strength. It also brings unity and encouragement, knowing that we are not alone but supported by a community of believers. As we pray for others, we grow in empathy and love, reflecting God's heart for His people.

FURTHER SCRIPTURE:

- James 5:16: Pray for one another, that you may be healed; the prayer of a righteous person is powerful.
- Ephesians 6:18: Pray in the Spirit on all occasions, with all kinds of prayers and requests.
- Colossians 1:9: Paul prays for the spiritual growth and knowledge of the Colossians.

PRAYER:

Lord, thank You for the privilege of interceding for others. Help me to be faithful in praying for my family, friends, and those in need. May my prayers be a source of encouragement and strength for them. Teach me to see others through Your eyes and to lift them up to You with compassion and faith. Amen.

PERSONAL REFLECTION:

Who are the people I need to pray for toDay? How can I make intercessory prayer a regular part of my prayer life?

DAY 41: PRAYING WITH THANKSGIVING

Scripture: Colossians 4:2 (NASB)
*"Devote yourselves to prayer, keeping alert in
it with an attitude of thanksgiving."*

ANECDOTE:

A grateful student writes a letter to his teacher, thanking her for her dedication and guidance. He acknowledges the impact she has had on his life, not just in academics but in character and personal growth. The act of expressing gratitude deepens his appreciation and fosters a sense of respect and love for his teacher.

APPLICATION:

Praying with thanksgiving is an essential part of our relationship with God. When we express gratitude in our prayers, we acknowledge God's goodness, faithfulness, and provision. Colossians 4:2 encourages believers to devote themselves to prayer with an attitude of thanksgiving. Thanksgiving shifts our focus from our problems to God's blessings, cultivating a heart of gratitude and contentment.

Praying with thanksgiving helps us to see God's hand at work in our lives, even in difficult circumstances. It reminds us of His past faithfulness, which strengthens our trust for the future. Gratitude in prayer also opens our eyes to the many ways God has blessed us, leading to joy and a positive outlook. By regularly thanking God in prayer, we develop a habit of recognizing and appreciating His presence and provision in every aspect of our lives.

FURTHER SCRIPTURE:

- 1 Thessalonians 5:18: Give thanks in all circumstances; for this is God's will for you in Christ Jesus.
- Philippians 4:6: Present your requests to God with thanksgiving.
- Psalm 100:4: Enter His gates with thanksgiving and His courts with praise.

PRAYER:

Lord, thank You for Your goodness and faithfulness. Thank You for the many blessings You have poured into my life. Help me to always come to You with a heart of gratitude, recognizing Your hand at work in every situation. May my prayers be filled with thanksgiving, bringing You the honor and praise You deserve. Amen.

PERSONAL REFLECTION:

What specific things am I grateful for toDay? How can I incorporate more thanksgiving into my daily prayer life?

DAY 42: LISTENING IN PRAYER

Scripture: Psalm 46:10 (NASB)
*"Be still, and know that I am God; I will be exalt-
ed among the nations, I will be exalted in the earth."*

ANECDOTE:

A busy executive decides to take a retreat in a quiet cabin in the woods. Away from the constant noise and demands of work, she finds peace in the silence. As she sits quietly, she becomes more attuned to the sounds of nature around her and begins to reflect on her life, gaining new insights and clarity. The stillness allows her to hear what she often misses in the hustle of daily life.

APPLICATION:

Prayer is not only about speaking to God but also about listening. Psalm 46:10 invites us to be still and know that God is God. In the stillness, we can hear His voice, sense His presence, and receive His guidance. Listening in prayer requires us to quiet our minds, set aside distractions, and focus on God. It involves being open to the Holy Spirit's promptings, allowing Him to speak to our hearts.

Listening in prayer deepens our relationship with God, making it a two-way conversation. It teaches us patience, humility, and dependence. By taking time to listen, we become more aware of God's leading in our decisions, relationships, and daily actions. Listening also brings peace, as we rest in the knowledge that God is in control. Developing the discipline of listening in prayer enhances our spiritual growth, making us more attuned to God's will and purpose.

FURTHER SCRIPTURE:

- 1 Kings 19:12: God speaks to Elijah in a gentle whisper.
- Isaiah 30:21: You will hear a voice behind you, saying, "This is the way; walk in it."
- John 10:27: Jesus says His sheep hear His voice, and He knows them.

PRAYER:

Lord, help me to be still and listen for Your voice. Teach me to quiet my mind and heart, setting aside the noise of daily life. I want to hear Your guidance and feel Your presence. Speak to me, Lord, and lead me in Your truth. May I be attentive to the Holy Spirit and responsive to Your direction. Amen.

PERSONAL REFLECTION:

How can I create more space in my life to listen to God in prayer? What practices can help me become more attuned to God's voice?

FIRMING UP YOUR FAITH
PRAYER

- What role does prayer play in your relationship with God, and how has it deepened this week?

- How can you use the Lord's Prayer as a model for your own prayer life?

- What does it mean to you to pray in faith and with persistence?

- Reflect on the importance of intercessory prayer. Who can you pray for this week?

- How can you incorporate thanksgiving and listening more fully into your prayers?

WEEK 7
THE CHURCH

DAY 43: THE CHURCH AS THE BODY OF CHRIST

Scripture: 1 Corinthians 12:27 (NASB)
"Now you are Christ's body, and individually members of it."

ANECDOTE:

A symphony orchestra comprises various instruments—violins, flutes, trumpets, and drums—each producing a unique sound. When played individually, they can make beautiful music, but when they play together in harmony, guided by a conductor, they create a magnificent symphony that resonates powerfully with the audience. Every instrument plays a crucial role, contributing to the overall masterpiece.

APPLICATION:

The Church is often referred to as the Body of Christ, a powerful metaphor that illustrates the unity and diversity within the community of believers. Each member of the church has a unique role to play, just as each part of a body has a specific function. Some may serve by teaching, others by providing hospitality, still others by offering encouragement or administration. Regardless of our specific role, each of us is essential to the health and mission of the church.

Being part of the Body of Christ means that we are interconnected; we need one another to grow and thrive. It's through relationships within the church that we experience love, support, and accountability. As we use our gifts to serve others, we build up the church and glorify God. This image of the body encourages us to embrace diversity and work together in unity, acknowledging that Christ is the head of the church, guiding us and empowering us to fulfill His mission.

FURTHER SCRIPTURE:

- Romans 12:4-5: Just as each of us has one body with many members, so in Christ, we form one body.
- Ephesians 4:11-13: Christ gave gifts to equip His people for works of service, building up the body.
- Colossians 1:18: Christ is the head of the body, the church.

PRAYER:

Lord, thank You for making me a part of the Body of Christ. Help me to recognize my role and use my gifts to serve and build up the church. Teach me to value and appreciate the diversity of gifts within the church community. May we work together in unity, reflecting Your love and fulfilling Your purpose. Amen.

PERSONAL REFLECTION:

What role do I play in the Body of Christ? How can I use my unique gifts to serve others and contribute to the church community?

DAY 44: THE FELLOWSHIP OF BELIEVERS

Scripture: Acts 2:42 (NASB)
"They were continually devoting themselves to the apostles' teaching and to fellowship, to the breaking of bread and to prayer."

ANECDOTE:

A charcoal fire is built with several pieces of coal placed together. Each piece contributes to the overall heat, making the fire strong and effective. If one piece of coal is removed and set aside, it quickly loses its heat and grows cold. However, when it is placed back with the others, it reignites, burning brightly once again.

APPLICATION:

The early church in Acts was characterized by a deep commitment to fellowship. Fellowship is more than just socializing; it's about building meaningful relationships centered on Christ. The believers devoted themselves to teaching, sharing meals, praying together, and supporting one another. This fellowship created a strong sense of community, where each person felt connected, cared for, and encouraged.

Fellowship is vital for spiritual growth and health. It provides a space for believers to share their struggles, celebrate victories, and bear one another's burdens. It is through fellowship that we experience love, acceptance, and encouragement. Being involved in a church community helps us stay spiritually vibrant and prevents us from becoming isolated and spiritually cold. Engaging in fellowship means being intentional about spending time with other believers, participating in small groups, attending church services, and investing in relationships that strengthen our faith. Through fellowship, we reflect the unity and love of Christ to the world.

FURTHER SCRIPTURE:

- Hebrews 10:24-25: Let us consider how to stir one another to love and good works, not neglecting to meet together.
- 1 John 1:7: If we walk in the light, as He is in the light, we have fellowship with one another.
- Ecclesiastes 4:9-10: Two are better than one, for they have a good return for their labor.

PRAYER:

Father, thank You for the gift of fellowship within the church. Help me to be devoted to building meaningful relationships with other believers. Teach me to be an encouragement and support to those around me, and may our fellowship reflect Your love and unity. Draw us closer together as we seek to grow in faith and serve one another. Amen.

PERSONAL REFLECTION:

How can I be more intentional about building and maintaining fellowship with other believers? What steps can I take to strengthen my connection to the church community?

DAY 45: THE GREAT COMMISSION

Scripture: Matthew 28:19-20 (NASB)
"Go therefore and make disciples of all the nations, baptiz-ing them in the name of the Father and the Son and the Holy Spirit, teaching them to observe all that I commanded you; and lo, I am with you always, even to the end of the age."

ANECDOTE:

A company CEO gives a final speech before retiring, outlining the vision and mission for the future. He emphasizes the importance of reaching new markets, expanding the company's influence, and staying true to the core values. The employees take his words to heart, knowing that this vision will guide their efforts and determine their success.

APPLICATION:

The Great Commission, given by Jesus before His ascension, is the mission and mandate for the church. Jesus commands His followers to go and make disciples of all nations, baptizing them and teaching them to observe His commands. This commission emphasizes the global scope of the gospel and the responsibility of every believer to be involved in sharing the message of Christ.

Making disciples involves evangelism (sharing the good news of Jesus) and discipleship (helping new believers grow in their faith). The church exists not only for worship and fellowship but also for mission. Jesus' promise to be with us always assures us that we do not carry out this mission alone; He empowers us through the Holy Spirit. The Great Commission challenges us to look beyond our immediate surroundings and to care about the spiritual well-being of people around the world. It calls us to be proactive in sharing our faith, supporting missions, and living out the teachings of Christ in our daily lives.

FURTHER SCRIPTURE:

- Acts 1:8: Jesus promises the Holy Spirit will empower believers to be His witnesses to the ends of the earth.
- Mark 16:15: Jesus tells His disciples to preach the gospel to all creation.
- Romans 10:14-15: How can people believe in the one they have not heard of? Faith comes from hearing the message.

PRAYER:

Lord Jesus, thank You for entrusting me with the Great Commission. Help me to be faithful in sharing the gospel and making disciples. Give me the courage to speak about my faith and the wisdom to guide others in their walk with You. May Your Spirit empower me, and may my life be a reflection of Your love and truth. Amen.

PERSONAL REFLECTION:

How can I be more involved in fulfilling the Great Commission? What opportunities do I have to share the gospel and disciple others in my community and beyond?

DAY 46: BAPTISM: AN OUTWARD EXPRESSION

Scripture: Romans 6:4 (NASB)

"Therefore we have been buried with Him through baptism into death, so that as Christ was raised from the dead through the glory of the Father, so we too might walk in newness of life."

ANECDOTE:

A person joins a sports team and is given a uniform. Putting on the uniform symbolizes their commitment to the team, their willingness to play by the team's rules, and their identification with the team's goals. The uniform is a visible sign of belonging and a declaration of participation.

APPLICATION:

Baptism is an important step of obedience and public declaration of faith in Jesus Christ. It symbolizes the believer's identification with Christ's death, burial, and resurrection. Just as Jesus died and was raised to new life, baptism represents the believer's death to sin and new life in Christ. It is an outward expression of an inward transformation, signifying repentance, forgiveness, and commitment to follow Jesus.

While baptism itself does not save, it is a powerful testimony of faith and a step of obedience to Christ's command. Being baptized is a way of publicly declaring allegiance to Jesus and identifying with the community of believers. It's an act of faith that says, "I belong to Christ, and I am committed to living for Him." Baptism also serves as a reminder of God's grace and the new life we have received through Jesus. It encourages us to walk in the newness of life, leaving behind the old ways and embracing the righteousness of Christ. Finally, Baptism is the first command of Christ Jesus to the believer. We should be baptized as soon as possible after confessing Christ as Lord.

FURTHER SCRIPTURE:

- Matthew 28:19: Jesus instructs His disciples to baptize in the name of the Father, Son, and Holy Spirit.
- Acts 2:38: Peter tells the crowd to repent and be baptized in the name of Jesus Christ for the forgiveness of sins.
- Colossians 2:12: We are buried with Christ in baptism and raised with Him through faith.

PRAYER:

Lord, I pray that I would be faithful in every way. Help me to not forget the price that you paid on the cross and to glory in your resurrection. In my baptism and my life I pray that I would always be a testimony to the goodness of God.

PERSONAL REFLECTION:

Have you been baptized as a follower of Christ? If not, I encourage you to be obedient to the Lord's command and demonstrate your love to Him in obedience.

DAY 47: LIVING BY FAITH IN COMMUNITY

Scripture: Galatians 6:2 (NASB)
"Bear one another's burdens, and thereby fulfill the law of Christ."

ANECDOTE:

Two friends set out on a long hike through rugged terrain. As they travel, one of them twists his ankle and struggles to continue. His friend immediately steps in, offering his shoulder for support and carrying some of his gear. Together, they navigate the challenging path, each encouraging the other along the way. By bearing the burden together, they reach their destination.

APPLICATION:

Living by faith is not something we are meant to do in isolation. God designed the church as a community where believers can support, encourage, and help each other. Paul's exhortation in Galatians to "bear one another's burdens" highlights the importance of empathy and shared responsibility within the church. Bearing burdens means coming alongside those who are struggling, offering practical help, prayer, and encouragement. It's an expression of love and compassion, reflecting the heart of Jesus.

In the church community, we find strength and support that we may not have on our own. Whether it's helping someone in financial need, providing a listening ear, or praying for someone facing illness, bearing burdens builds unity and deepens relationships. It also fulfills the law of Christ, which is to love one another as He has loved us. As we share in each other's joys and sorrows, we grow stronger in faith and more closely reflect the image of Christ to the world.

FURTHER SCRIPTURE:

- Romans 12:15: Rejoice with those who rejoice; mourn with those who mourn.
- 1 Thessalonians 5:11: Encourage one another and build each other up.
- John 13:34-35: Jesus commands us to love one another as He has loved us.

PRAYER:

Lord, thank You for the gift of community and the support of fellow believers. Help me to be sensitive to the needs of those around me and to bear their burdens with compassion and love. Teach me to serve selflessly, reflecting Your love to those in need. May our church be a place of healing, encouragement, and unity. Amen.

PERSONAL REFLECTION:

How can I be more proactive in supporting and encouraging others within my church community? What specific actions can I take to help bear the burdens of those around me?

DAY 48: THE POWER OF UNITY IN THE CHURCH

Scripture: Ephesians 4:3 (NASB)
"Being diligent to preserve the unity of the Spirit in the bond of peace."

ANECDOTE:

A team of rowers participates in a race. Each rower has a specific role and must pull in unison with the others for the boat to move swiftly and efficiently. If one rower is out of sync, the boat slows down and becomes harder to steer. But when they work together, the boat glides smoothly through the water, propelled by their combined effort and unity.

APPLICATION:

Unity is a powerful force within the church, essential for fulfilling God's purposes. Paul's exhortation to the Ephesians emphasizes the importance of preserving the unity of the Spirit. Unity doesn't mean uniformity; it means working together harmoniously, despite differences, to achieve a common goal. It involves humility, patience, and love, recognizing that each member of the church has unique gifts and perspectives that contribute to the whole.

Preserving unity requires effort and intentionality. It means resolving conflicts quickly, forgiving one another, and putting the needs of others before our own. When the church is united, it reflects the nature of God, who is one, and it becomes a powerful witness to the world. Unity in the church promotes peace, fosters growth, and creates an environment where the Holy Spirit can work freely. As believers, we are called to be peacemakers, actively seeking to build bridges, encourage understanding, and maintain the bond of peace.

FURTHER SCRIPTURE:

- Psalm 133:1: How good and pleasant it is when God's people live together in unity.
- Colossians 3:14: Love binds everything together in perfect unity.
- John 17:21: Jesus prays for all believers to be one, just as He and the Father are one.

PRAYER:

Heavenly Father, thank You for the unity we have through the Spirit. Help me to be diligent in preserving this unity within my church. Teach me to be patient, humble, and loving toward others, even when we disagree. May our church be a beacon of peace and a testimony of Your love to the world. Unite us in purpose and mission, so that we may glorify You in all we do. Amen.

PERSONAL REFLECTION:

What steps can I take to promote unity within my church? How can I contribute to an environment of peace and cooperation among fellow believers?

DAY 49: THE LORD'S SUPPER

Scripture: 1 Corinthians 11:23-26 (NASB)

"For I received from the Lord that which I also delivered to you, that the Lord Jesus in the night in which He was betrayed took bread; and when He had given thanks, He broke it and said, 'This is My body, which is for you; do this in remembrance of Me.' In the same way, He took the cup also after supper, saying, 'This cup is the new covenant in My blood; do this, as often as you drink it, in remembrance of Me.' For as often as you eat this bread and drink the cup, you proclaim the Lord's death until He comes."

ANECDOTE:

Imagine a family gathering for a special meal to remember a loved one. As they eat together, they share stories and memories, celebrating the life and legacy of the person they honor. Each meal becomes a way to keep the memory alive, reinforcing the bond they share and reminding them of the love that unites them.

APPLICATION:

The Lord's Supper, also known as Communion, is a sacred practice instituted by Jesus on the night He was betrayed. This meal serves as a powerful reminder of Jesus' sacrificial death, His body broken, and His blood shed for the forgiveness of our sins. It's a time to remember His love, reflect on His sacrifice, and renew our commitment to Him. As believers, participating in the Lord's Supper is a proclamation of our faith in Jesus' atoning work on the cross and our hope in His return.

When we partake in the Lord's Supper, we are not just remembering a historical event; we are entering into a deeper communion with Christ and with one another. This act symbolizes the new covenant established through Jesus' blood, a covenant that offers forgiveness, redemption, and reconciliation with God. It's a time of self-examination, repentance, and gratitude, acknowledging the grace that has been extended to us through Jesus' sacrifice.

The Lord's Supper also serves as a reminder of our unity as the body of Christ. As we eat the bread and drink from the cup, we remember that we are one in Christ, called to love and serve one another. This meal is not just a ritual; it's a meaningful expression of our faith and our shared commitment to follow Jesus. Let us approach the Lord's Supper with reverence, gratitude, and a heart open to His transforming grace.

FURTHER SCRIPTURE:

- Matthew 26:26-28: Jesus institutes the Lord's Supper, saying, "Take, eat; this is My body."
- Luke 22:19-20: Jesus says, "Do this in remembrance of Me."
- John 6:53-54: Jesus speaks of the importance of eating His flesh and drinking His blood to have eternal life.

PRAYER:

Lord Jesus, thank You for the gift of the Lord's Supper, a powerful reminder of Your sacrifice and love. Help me to approach this sacred meal with reverence and gratitude, remembering all that You have done for me. May it be a time of renewal, reflection, and a deepening of my relationship with You. Strengthen my faith and unite me with my fellow believers as we proclaim Your death and resurrection until You come again. Amen.

PERSONAL REFLECTION:

What does the Lord's Supper mean to me? How can I prepare my heart to participate in this sacred meal with a deeper sense of gratitude and commitment to Christ?

FIRMING UP YOUR FAITH
THE CHURCH

- How does viewing the church as the body of Christ influence your role within it?

- What steps can you take to foster deeper fellowship with other believers?

- Reflect on the Great Commission and your role in fulfilling it.

- How can baptism and the Lord's Supper become more meaningful in your spiritual life?

- In what ways can you serve others within your local church community

WEEK 8
CHRISTIAN LIVING

DAY 50: LIVING BY FAITH

Scripture: Hebrews 11:1 (NASB)
*"Now faith is the assurance of things hoped
for, the conviction of things not seen."*

ANECDOTE:

A tightrope walker sets up a high wire across a deep canyon. As spectators gather, he confidently steps out onto the wire, balancing carefully with each step. The crowd watches in awe as he moves forward, trusting the wire to hold him despite the height and danger. His confidence in the wire and his own training keeps him focused and steady.

APPLICATION:

Living by faith means trusting God even when we cannot see the outcome. Hebrews 11:1 defines faith as assurance and conviction in things hoped for but not yet seen. Faith is not just a mental belief; it's a confident trust in God's promises, character, and faithfulness. It requires us to step out in obedience, relying on God's guidance, even when we don't understand His plans or see the full picture.

Living by faith involves surrendering our fears, doubts, and control to God. It means trusting that He is working for our good, even in difficult circumstances. Faith grows as we experience God's faithfulness over time, seeing how He has provided, protected, and guided us. It's through faith that we please God; we rely on His strength and wisdom rather than our own. Living by faith brings peace and joy, knowing that God is with us and that He is faithful to fulfill His promises.

FURTHER SCRIPTURE:

- 2 Corinthians 5:7: We walk by faith, not by sight.
- Romans 1:17: The righteous shall live by faith.
- Proverbs 3:5-6: Trust in the Lord with all your heart and lean not on your own understanding.

PRAYER:

Lord, help me to live by faith, trusting in Your promises and character. Strengthen my faith and help me to rely on You, especially when I cannot see the way ahead. Thank You for Your faithfulness and love. May my life be a testimony of faith that brings glory to You. Amen.

PERSONAL REFLECTION:

What areas of my life do I need to surrender to God in faith? How can I practice living by faith daily, trusting God's guidance and provision?

DAY 51: OBEDIENCE TO GOD

Scripture: John 14:15 (NASB)
"If you love Me, you will keep My commandments."

ANECDOTE:

A young apprentice in a bakery follows the instructions of his master baker precisely. He knows that his success depends on his willingness to learn and obey. Over time, as he faithfully follows the master's guidance, he becomes skilled in his craft, producing bread that is just as good as the master's, much to the delight of customers.

APPLICATION:

Obedience is a fundamental aspect of the Christian life. Jesus clearly states that our love for Him is demonstrated through our obedience to His commands. Obedience is not about following rules for the sake of following rules, it's about aligning our lives with God's will and reflecting His character. When we obey God, we show that we trust His wisdom, believe in His goodness, and desire to please Him.

Obedience often requires us to go against our natural inclinations, cultural norms, or personal desires. It calls us to humility, surrendering our own will in favor of God's. Obedience is also about consistency—choosing to follow God's Word in both big and small things. As we practice obedience, we grow in maturity and become more like Christ. It's through obedience that we experience the blessings of God's guidance, protection, and provision. Obedience leads to a deeper relationship with God, as we learn to hear His voice and follow His lead.

FURTHER SCRIPTURE:

- James 1:22: Be doers of the word, and not hearers only, deceiving yourselves.
- 1 Samuel 15:22: To obey is better than sacrifice, and to heed is better than the fat of rams.
- Deuteronomy 28:1-2: Obey the Lord your God, and blessings will come upon you.

PRAYER:

Lord, I desire to obey You in all things. Help me to hear Your voice clearly and to follow Your commands with a willing heart. Teach me to trust in Your wisdom and to surrender my will to Yours. May my obedience be a reflection of my love for You, and may it lead me closer to Your heart. Amen.

PERSONAL REFLECTION:

Are there areas in my life where I struggle with obedience? How can I take practical steps to align my actions with God's commands and demonstrate my love for Him?

DAY 52: LOVING GOD AND OTHERS

Scripture: Matthew 22:37-39 (NASB)
"And He said to him, 'You shall love the Lord your God with all your heart, and with all your soul, and with all your mind.' This is the great and foremost commandment. The second is like it, 'You shall love your neighbor as yourself.'"

ANECDOTE:

A gardener tends his garden with great care, watering the plants, removing weeds, and ensuring they receive plenty of sunlight. His attention and love for the garden result in beautiful, vibrant flowers that bring joy to everyone who sees them. His love for his garden is evident in the health and beauty of the plants.

APPLICATION:

Jesus summarized the entire law with two commandments: to love God with all our heart, soul, mind and strength, and to love our neighbor as ourselves. Love is the foundation of the Christian life and the greatest mark of a true follower of Christ. Loving God means putting Him first in all things, seeking to know Him more, worshiping Him sincerely, and living in a way that honors Him. This love for God flows out into love for others.

Loving others involves showing kindness, compassion, and grace, just as God has shown us. It means putting the needs of others before our own, forgiving when we are wronged, and serving those in need. Love is not just a feeling; it is an action. It is a choice we make daily, often in small but significant ways. As we love God and others we fulfill the law of Christ and reflect His character to the world. This love builds strong relationships, creates community, and draws people closer to God.

FURTHER SCRIPTURE:

- 1 John 4:19: We love because He first loved us.
- Romans 13:9-10: Love does no wrong to a neighbor; therefore, love is the fulfillment of the law.
- 1 Corinthians 13:13: And now these three remain: faith, hope, and love. But the greatest of these is love.

PRAYER:

Heavenly Father, teach me to love You with all my heart, soul, and mind. Help me to prioritize my relationship with You above all else. Show me how to love others as You have loved me, with kindness, compassion, and grace. May my love be a testimony of Your presence in my life, drawing others to You. Amen.

PERSONAL REFLECTION:

How can I grow in my love for God and make Him the priority in my life? What practical ways can I show love to those around me toDay?

DAY 53: WALKING IN HUMILITY

Scripture: Philippians 2:3 (NASB)

"Do nothing from selfishness or empty conceit, but with humility of mind regard one another as more important than yourselves."

ANECDOTE:

A successful leader is known for his humility. Despite his achievements, he treats everyone with respect, listens to their ideas, and acknowledges their contributions. His humility fosters a positive environment, encouraging teamwork and collaboration. People respect and admire him, not just for his success, but for his character and the way he treats others.

APPLICATION:

Humility is a key virtue in the Christian life, modeled perfectly by Jesus, who humbled Himself by becoming human and dying on the cross. Paul encourages believers to do nothing out of selfishness but to consider others more important than themselves. Humility is not about thinking less of ourselves but thinking of ourselves less. It's about recognizing that we are all equal before God and valuing others' needs and perspectives.

Walking in humility means being willing to serve others, even when it's inconvenient or goes unnoticed. It involves admitting our mistakes, being teachable, and giving credit to others. Humility fosters unity, builds strong relationships, and creates an environment where people feel valued and respected. It also opens the door for God's grace, as He gives grace to the humble but opposes the proud (James 4:6). As we walk in humility, we reflect the character of Christ and bring glory to God.

FURTHER SCRIPTURE:

- Micah 6:8: He has shown you what is good—to act justly, love mercy, and walk humbly with your God.
- Matthew 23:12: Whoever exalts himself will be humbled, and whoever humbles himself will be exalted.
- 1 Peter 5:5: Clothe yourselves with humility toward one another.

PRAYER:

Lord Jesus, thank You for the example of humility You set for us. Help me to walk in humility, considering others more important than myself. Help me to serve others with humility and to have a teachable spirit. May I be a reflection of you in all things and bring God glory and honor.

PERSONAL REFLECTION:

How can you take the spiritual gifts the Holy Spirit has given you and serve others? Allow the Holy Spirit to search your heart and see if there is any prideful way in you.

DAY 54: FORGIVING OTHERS

Scripture: Ephesians 4:32 (NASB)
*"Be kind to one another, tender-hearted, forgiving each
other, just as God in Christ also has forgiven you."*

ANECDOTE:

A teacher notices a conflict between two students in her class. One of them accidentally broke the other's favorite toy. The upset child demanded an apology but refused to forgive, holding onto anger throughout the Day. Seeing the tension, the teacher called them both aside, reminding them of the times they had each needed forgiveness. The offended child softened, realizing that holding a grudge was only making them both unhappy. They decided to forgive, and peace was restored.

APPLICATION:

Forgiveness is a powerful act of grace that reflects God's character. In Ephesians 4:32, Paul calls believers to be kind, tender-hearted, and forgiving, just as God has forgiven us through Christ. Forgiveness is not always easy; it often requires us to let go of hurt and resentment. However, forgiveness is essential for our spiritual and emotional health. Holding onto unforgiveness can lead to bitterness, anger, and division, while forgiveness brings healing, restoration, and peace.

Forgiving others doesn't mean excusing wrong behavior or ignoring injustice. It means releasing the offense to God, trusting Him to bring justice and healing. It involves seeking reconciliation when possible and allowing God's love to overcome hurt. Remembering how much God has forgiven us motivates us to extend forgiveness to others. Forgiveness is a choice, a decision to walk in freedom and love, reflecting the heart of Christ. By choosing to forgive, we break the chains of bitterness and open the door to God's grace in our lives.

FURTHER SCRIPTURE:

- Matthew 6:14-15: Jesus teaches that if we forgive others, our heavenly Father will also forgive us.
- Colossians 3:13: Forgive as the Lord forgave you.
- Luke 23:34: Jesus forgives those who crucified Him, saying, "Father, forgive them."

PRAYER:

Lord, thank You for the forgiveness You have given me through Jesus. Help me to forgive others with the same grace and love. Soften my heart and remove any bitterness or anger. Teach me to walk in kindness and compassion, reflecting Your mercy to those around me. May my forgiveness bring healing and peace, and may it glorify You. Amen.

PERSONAL REFLECTION:

Is there someone I need to forgive toDay? How can I take a step toward forgiveness and let go of any bitterness or hurt?

DAY 55: BEARING FRUIT FOR GOD

Scripture: John 15:5 (NASB)
"I am the vine, you are the branches; he who abides in Me and I in him, he bears much fruit, for apart from Me you can do nothing."

ANECDOTE:

A gardener tends to his vineyard, ensuring each vine is well-nourished and pruned. He knows that a healthy vine will produce an abundant harvest of grapes. One Day he notices a branch that is disconnected from the vine, lying on the ground. Without the connection to the vine, the branch withers, unable to bear fruit. The gardener takes care to remove dead branches, allowing the healthy ones to thrive and bear much fruit.

APPLICATION:

Bearing fruit is a natural outcome of abiding in Christ. Jesus describes Himself as the vine and believers as the branches. When we remain connected to Him through prayer, reading His Word, and living in obedience, we bear fruit that reflects His character. This fruit includes love, joy, peace, patience, kindness, goodness, faithfulness, gentleness, and self-control, often referred to as the fruit of the Spirit (Galatians 5:22-23).

Fruit-bearing is not about our own efforts; it is the result of Christ's life flowing through us. When we abide in Him, His Spirit works in and through us, producing spiritual fruit that blesses others and glorifies God. Bearing fruit also involves leading others to Christ, serving with our gifts, and making a positive impact on the world around us. By staying connected to Jesus, we find the strength, guidance, and nourishment we need to live fruitful lives. Apart from Him, we can do nothing of eternal value.

FURTHER SCRIPTURE:

- Galatians 5:22-23: The fruit of the Spirit includes love, joy, peace, patience, kindness, goodness, faithfulness, gentleness, and self-control.
- Matthew 7:17-20: A good tree bears good fruit; a bad tree bears bad fruit.
- Colossians 1:10: Walk in a manner worthy of the Lord, bearing fruit in every good work.

PRAYER:

Lord Jesus, help me to abide in You each Day. May Your life flow through me, producing fruit that reflects Your character and brings glory to God. Teach me to remain in Your love, to walk in obedience, and to be open to the work of the Holy Spirit. May my life bear much fruit, impacting others for Your kingdom. Amen.

PERSONAL REFLECTION:

What does it mean for me to abide in Christ daily? How can I cultivate a lifestyle that bears spiritual fruit and reflects God's love to others?

DAY 56: PERSEVERING IN TRIALS

Scripture: James 1:2-4 (NASB)
"Consider it all joy, my brethren, when you encounter various trials, knowing that the testing of your faith produces endurance. And let endurance have its perfect result, so that you may be perfect and complete, lacking in nothing."

ANECDOTE:

A marathon runner faces many challenges along the race route: steep hills, fatigue, and muscle cramps. But with each step, he focuses on the finish line and the satisfaction of completing the race. He knows that perseverance is key, and each challenge he overcomes builds his strength and endurance, making him a better runner.

APPLICATION:

Perseverance is an essential part of the Christian life, especially in times of trials and challenges. James encourages believers to consider it joy when facing trials because these experiences test our faith and produce endurance. Trials are opportunities for growth, strengthening our character, and deepening our dependence on God. They refine our faith, teaching us to trust God more fully and rely on His strength.

Perseverance means holding on to our faith, even when circumstances are difficult or when we don't understand why things are happening. It's about choosing to keep moving forward, trusting that God is with us and has a purpose for our trials. As we persevere we become mature, complete, and better equipped to handle future challenges. Perseverance also serves as a powerful testimony to others, showing the strength and resilience that comes from a life anchored in Christ. By enduring through trials, we reflect God's faithfulness and inspire others to do the same.

FURTHER SCRIPTURE:

- Romans 5:3-4: Suffering produces perseverance; perseverance, character; and character, hope.
- 1 Peter 1:6-7: Trials test the genuineness of your faith, which is more precious than gold.
- Hebrews 12:1: Let us run with endurance the race that is set before us.

PRAYER:

Father, thank You for Your presence in times of trials. Help me to persevere with faith and joy, knowing that You are working in me and through me. Give me the strength to endure, the wisdom to learn from my challenges, and the peace that comes from trusting in You. May my perseverance bring glory to Your name and inspire others to trust You. Amen.

PERSONAL REFLECTION:

What trials am I currently facing, and how can I choose to persevere with faith? How can I encourage others who may be going through difficult times to hold on to their faith.

FIRMING UP YOUR FAITH
CHRISTIAN LIVING

- How has living by faith shaped your approach to life's challenges?

- In what areas is God calling you to greater obedience?

- Reflect on Jesus' command to love God and others. How can you put this into practice?

- How does walking in humility and forgiveness transform your relationships?

- What does it mean to bear fruit for God, and how can you persevere through trials?

WEEK 9
SPIRITUAL WARFARE

DAY 57: UNDERSTANDING SPIRITUAL WARFARE

Scripture: Ephesians 6:12 (NASB)
"For our struggle is not against flesh and blood, but against the rulers, against the powers, against the world forces of this darkness, against the spiritual forces of wickedness in the heavenly places."

ANECDOTE:

A soldier prepares for battle, knowing that the real enemy is not just the people on the other side but the strategies, tactics, and unseen forces working against him. He understands that victory requires more than physical strength; it requires awareness, strategy, and the right equipment to counteract the enemy's moves.

APPLICATION:

Spiritual warfare is a reality for every believer. Paul reminds us in Ephesians that our struggle is not against flesh and blood—meaning our battle is not with people but with spiritual forces of evil. These forces operate in ways that are often unseen, influencing thoughts, actions, and circumstances. Understanding spiritual warfare is crucial because it helps us recognize that the challenges we face are not just physical or emotional but spiritual.

Recognizing spiritual warfare changes how we approach conflicts, temptations, and trials. It calls us to be vigilant, aware of the enemy's tactics, and dependent on God's power. Spiritual warfare involves prayer, standing firm in faith, and using the spiritual weapons God has provided. Knowing we are in a spiritual battle encourages us to stay close to God, relying on His guidance and protection. It also reminds us that victory is possible through Christ, who has already overcome the enemy.

FURTHER SCRIPTURE:

- 1 Peter 5:8: Be sober-minded; be watchful. Your adversary the devil prowls around like a roaring lion.
- 2 Corinthians 10:3-4: Though we live in the world, we do not wage war as the world does.
- James 4:7: Submit to God, resist the devil, and he will flee from you.

PRAYER:

Lord, open my eyes to the reality of spiritual warfare. Help me to recognize the enemy's tactics and to stand firm in my faith. Teach me to rely on Your strength and to use the spiritual weapons You have provided. Protect me from the schemes of the enemy, and guide me in truth. Amen.

PERSONAL REFLECTION:

What areas of my life might be under spiritual attack? How can I be more vigilant and prepared for spiritual warfare?

DAY 58: RECOGNIZING THE ENEMY

Scripture: John 10:10 (NASB)
"The thief comes only to steal and kill and destroy; I came that they may have life, and have it abundantly."

ANECDOTE:

A homeowner installs a security system after realizing there have been burglaries in the neighborhood. Knowing the enemy's goal is to steal and harm, the homeowner takes precautions, staying vigilant and alert to any signs of intrusion. By recognizing the threat, he can protect his home and family more effectively.

APPLICATION:

The Bible makes it clear that we have an enemy—Satan—who seeks to steal, kill, and destroy. Jesus contrasts the enemy's destructive intentions with His own purpose of giving life abundantly. Recognizing the enemy's strategies is the first step in defending against spiritual attacks. Satan often uses deception, temptation, doubt, fear, and accusations to disrupt our relationship with God and derail our spiritual growth.

Recognizing the enemy means being aware of the ways he tries to influence our thoughts, emotions, and actions. It involves identifying lies, resisting temptation, and standing firm in God's truth. We must be careful not to underestimate the enemy, but also not to live in fear. Our victory is secure in Christ, who has defeated Satan through His death and resurrection. By staying close to Jesus, immersing ourselves in His Word, and praying for discernment, we can recognize the enemy's tactics and stand strong against them.

FURTHER SCRIPTURE:

- 2 Corinthians 11:14: Satan disguises himself as an angel of light.
- 1 John 3:8: The Son of God appeared to destroy the works of the devil.
- Revelation 12:10: Satan is the accuser of the brethren.

PRAYER:

Lord Jesus, help me to recognize the enemy's tactics and to stand firm in Your truth. Protect me from deception and temptation. Give me discernment to see through the lies of the enemy, and remind me of the abundant life You have promised. Strengthen my faith, and help me to live in the victory You have won. Amen.

PERSONAL REFLECTION:

How have I seen the enemy's tactics at work in my life? What steps can I take to guard against his schemes and live in the fullness of God's truth?

DAY 59: THE ARMOR OF GOD

Scripture: Ephesians 6:13 (NASB)
*"Therefore, take up the full armor of God, so that you will be able
to resist in the evil day, and having done everything, to stand firm."*

ANECDOTE:

A firefighter suits up before entering a burning building. Each piece of his gear—from the helmet to the boots—serves a specific purpose, protecting him from heat, smoke, and falling debris. Without his gear, he would be vulnerable and at great risk. But with the full armor, he is equipped to face the dangers and rescue those in need.

APPLICATION:

Paul instructs believers to put on the full armor of God to stand against the enemy's attacks. The armor of God includes the belt of truth, the breastplate of righteousness, the shoes of peace, the shield of faith, the helmet of salvation, and the sword of the Spirit (Ephesians 6:14-17). Each piece of armor represents a spiritual truth and defense against the enemy's tactics.

The belt of truth helps us stand firm in God's truth, countering the lies and deceptions of the enemy. The breastplate of righteousness protects our hearts, reminding us of our identity in Christ and His righteousness that covers us. The shoes of peace equip us to stand firm and share the gospel of peace. The shield of faith extinguishes the fiery darts of doubt, fear, and temptation. The helmet of salvation guards our minds, giving us assurance of our salvation. The sword of the Spirit, which is the Word of God, is our offensive weapon, allowing us to fight back with God's truth.

Putting on the full armor of God is a daily practice of prayer, Scripture reading, and reliance on the Holy Spirit. It prepares us to face spiritual battles with confidence, knowing that God has equipped us for victory.

FURTHER SCRIPTURE:

- 1 Thessalonians 5:8: Put on faith and love as a breastplate and the hope of salvation as a helmet.
- Romans 13:12: Put aside the deeds of darkness and put on the armor of light.
- Isaiah 59:17: God wears righteousness as a breastplate and a helmet of salvation on His head.

PRAYER:

Father, help me to put on the full armor of God each Day. Equip me with Your truth, righteousness, peace, faith, salvation, and the Word of God. Strengthen me to stand firm against the enemy's attacks and to live boldly for You. May Your armor protect me and guide me in every battle I face. Amen.

PERSONAL REFLECTION:

Which piece of the armor of God do I need to focus on in my life right now? How can I incorporate putting on the full armor of God into my daily routine?

DAY 60: THE POWER OF PRAYER IN SPIRITUAL WARFARE

Scripture: Ephesians 6:18 (NASB)
"With all prayer and petition pray at all times in the Spirit, and with this in view, be on the alert with all perseverance and petition for all the saints."

ANECDOTE:

A soldier in battle relies on a radio to communicate with his command center, receiving instructions, updates, and support. Without this line of communication, he would be isolated, vulnerable, and at risk of making critical mistakes. The radio connection keeps him connected, informed, and prepared for whatever comes his way.

APPLICATION:

Prayer is a vital weapon in spiritual warfare. After describing the armor of God, Paul emphasizes the importance of praying at all times in the Spirit. Prayer connects us with God, aligning our hearts with His will, and inviting His power and presence into our battles. Through prayer, we find strength, guidance, and protection. It is through prayer that we resist the enemy, intercede for others, and remain vigilant in our faith.

Praying in the Spirit means being sensitive to the Holy Spirit's leading, allowing Him to guide our prayers according to God's will. It involves praying with perseverance, not giving up, even when we face challenges. Prayer covers us and others in God's protection, making us aware of spiritual realities and equipping us to stand firm. The power of prayer is not in our words but in the God who hears and responds. By praying continually, we remain alert and ready for any attack the enemy may bring.

FURTHER SCRIPTURE:

- 1 Thessalonians 5:17: Pray without ceasing.
- Philippians 4:6-7: Do not be anxious, but in everything by prayer and petition, present your requests to God.
- Matthew 26:41: Watch and pray so that you will not fall into temptation.

PRAYER:

Heavenly Father, I thank You for the gift of prayer, through which I can communicate with You and seek Your guidance and strength. Help me to pray continually and to be sensitive to the leading of Your Spirit. Teach me to be vigilant and persistent in prayer, interceding not only for my own needs but also for the needs of others. Strengthen me in the midst of spiritual battles, and help me to rely on Your power rather than my own. May my prayers be a source of strength, protection, and encouragement for myself and others. Amen.

PERSONAL REFLECTION:

How can I deepen my prayer life to be more effective in spiritual warfare? What specific things can I pray for to stand against the enemy's attacks and support others in their battles?

DAY 61: RELYING ON GOD'S STRENGTH

Scripture: Ephesians 6:10 (NASB)
"Finally, be strong in the Lord and in the strength of His might."

ANECDOTE:

A young athlete trains for a marathon. Despite his rigorous practice, he knows he cannot complete the race on his own strength alone. On race Day, his family and friends come out to cheer him on. Their encouragement boosts his energy, reminding him that he is not running alone. Every cheer and word of support gives him the strength to push forward, especially during the toughest parts of the race.

APPLICATION:

In spiritual warfare, relying on our own strength is not enough. Paul urges believers to be strong in the Lord and in the strength of His might. This command reminds us that our strength comes from God, not from ourselves. We face spiritual battles that require more than human effort; they require divine power. God's strength is made perfect in our weakness, and His might empowers us to stand firm against the enemy's attacks.

Relying on God's strength means acknowledging our dependence on Him and seeking His power through prayer, worship, and the study of His Word. It involves surrendering our fears and trusting that God is fighting for us. When we feel weak or discouraged, we can remember that God's strength is unlimited, and He is able to do immeasurably more than we ask or imagine. As we rely on His strength, we find courage, perseverance, and the ability to overcome any challenge. Our victories are not by our might, but by God's Spirit working in and through us.

FURTHER SCRIPTURE:

- Philippians 4:13: I can do all things through Him who strengthens me.
- 2 Corinthians 12:9: My grace is sufficient for you, for My power is made perfect in weakness.
- Isaiah 40:29: He gives strength to the weary and increases the power of the weak.

PRAYER:

Lord, I recognize that my strength is not enough for the battles I face. I rely on Your strength and power to stand firm and overcome. Fill me with Your might and help me to trust in Your ability to protect and guide me. Thank You for being my source of strength. May I live each Day depending on You, knowing that with You, I can face anything. Amen.

PERSONAL REFLECTION:

In what areas of my life do I need to rely more on God's strength? How can I practice seeking His power and presence in my daily spiritual battles?

DAY 62: CELEBRATING VICTORY IN CHRIST

Scripture: 1 Corinthians 15:57 (NASB)
"But thanks be to God, who gives us the victory through our Lord Jesus Christ."

ANECDOTE:

A football team trains tirelessly for the championship game. After months of preparation and hard-fought battles on the field, the final whistle blows, and they realize they have won. The players celebrate joyfully, hugging each other, lifting the trophy high, and thanking their coach for his guidance and support throughout the season. Their victory is a shared celebration, a testament to their teamwork and commitment.

APPLICATION:

As believers, we have reason to celebrate because victory is already ours through Jesus Christ. Paul's words in 1 Corinthians remind us to give thanks to God, who grants us victory over sin, death, and the enemy. This victory was secured through Jesus' death and resurrection. Because He triumphed over the grave, we share in His victory and have the assurance of eternal life.

Celebrating victory in Christ means living with joy, confidence, and hope. It means praising God for His faithfulness and acknowledging His power in every situation. Even when we face challenges we can hold onto the truth that the ultimate victory has been won. Our daily battles are real, but they do not define our final outcome. By focusing on Christ's victory, we find strength to persevere, courage to face opposition, and peace to overcome fear. Celebrating victory is not just about looking back at what God has done but also looking forward to the promises He has yet to fulfill.

FURTHER SCRIPTURE:

- Romans 8:37: In all these things, we are more than conquerors through Him who loved us.
- John 16:33: In this world, you will have trouble, but take heart! I have overcome the world.
- Revelation 12:11: They triumphed over him by the blood of the Lamb and by the word of their testimony.

PRAYER:

Heavenly Father, thank You for the victory You have given me through Jesus Christ. I praise You for Your faithfulness and power. Help me to live in the joy and confidence of this victory, knowing that no challenge is too great for You. May my life be a celebration of Your love, grace, and triumph. Strengthen my faith and help me to share the hope of victory with others. Amen.

DAY 63: STANDING ON GOD'S PROMISES

Scripture: Psalm 91:14-15 (NASB)
*"Because he has loved Me, therefore I will deliver him; I will
set him securely on high, because he has known My name.
He will call upon Me, and I will answer him; I will be
with him in trouble; I will rescue him and honor him."*

ANECDOTE:

A child holds tightly to a promise from his parent, trusting completely that it will be fulfilled. Even when others doubt or circumstances seem to contradict, the child's confidence remains unshaken because he knows his parent's character and faithfulness. This trust brings him peace, no matter what comes his way.

APPLICATION:

In the midst of spiritual warfare, God's promises are our sure foundation. Psalm 91:14-15 reminds us of God's commitment to protect and deliver those who love Him and know His name. God promises to be with us in trouble, to rescue us, and to honor us. These promises are not based on our strength or ability but on God's faithfulness and love. Standing on God's promises means trusting in His Word and holding onto His truth, even when circumstances are challenging or when we feel overwhelmed.

When we know God's promises, we can face spiritual battles with confidence, knowing that God is for us and will not abandon us. His promises give us hope, strengthen our faith, and provide the courage to persevere. Standing on God's promises involves regularly reading and meditating on Scripture, reminding ourselves of His faithfulness, and declaring His Word over our lives. As we stand on God's promises, we find peace and assurance, knowing that God is with us, fighting on our behalf.

FURTHER SCRIPTURE:

- Joshua 1:9: Be strong and courageous; do not be afraid, for the Lord your God is with you wherever you go.
- Isaiah 41:10: Do not fear, for I am with you; do not anxiously look about you, for I am your God.
- Romans 8:31: If God is for us, who can be against us?

PRAYER:

Lord, I thank You for the precious promises You have given me. Help me to stand firm on Your Word and trust in Your faithfulness. When I face spiritual battles, remind me of Your presence and Your commitment to protect and deliver me. Strengthen my faith and give me the courage to hold onto Your promises, no matter what challenges come my way. May Your promises be my shield and my hope. Amen.

PERSONAL REFLECTION:

What are some specific promises from God's Word that I can hold onto during spiritual battles? How can I remind myself daily of God's faithfulness and His commitment to protect and deliver me?

FIRMING UP YOUR FAITH
SPIRITUAL WARFARE

- How has this week's focus on spiritual warfare changed your view of the unseen battles we face?

- How can you effectively put on the armor of God in your daily life?

- In what ways can prayer be a powerful tool in spiritual warfare?

- How does faith equip you to resist temptation and overcome the enemy?

- What does it mean to live in victory in Christ, even amid struggles?

WEEK 10
THE HOLY SPIRIT

DAY 64: THE PROMISE OF THE HOLY SPIRIT

Scripture: John 14:16-17 (NASB)

"I will ask the Father, and He will give you another Helper, that He may be with you forever; that is the Spirit of truth, whom the world cannot receive, because it does not see Him or know Him, but you know Him because He abides with you and will be in you."

ANECDOTE:

A traveler on a long journey is given a guidebook and a map. Although it is helpful he still feels lost at times. Then, a guide joins him, offering to lead the way. The traveler's anxiety fades, replaced by confidence. With the guide by his side, he knows he will reach his destination safely. The guide not only shows the way but also teaches and comforts him during difficult parts of the journey.

APPLICATION:

Before Jesus ascended to heaven, He promised His disciples that He would send the Holy Spirit, referred to as the Helper or Comforter. The Holy Spirit is God's gift to every believer, dwelling within us and empowering us to live the Christian life. The Holy Spirit is the Spirit of truth, guiding us into all truth and helping us understand God's Word. His presence assures us that we are never alone, no matter what we face.

The promise of the Holy Spirit means we have a constant companion, teacher, and advocate. He comforts us in times of sorrow, gives us strength in times of weakness, and leads us in making decisions. The Holy Spirit's indwelling presence brings peace, joy, and assurance of God's love. As believers, we are called to be aware of the Holy Spirit's presence and to rely on His guidance daily. This requires a heart that is open, obedient, and sensitive to His leading. By trusting in the Holy Spirit, we experience the fullness of God's presence and power in our lives.

FURTHER SCRIPTURE:

- Acts 2:38: Peter tells the crowd to repent and receive the gift of the Holy Spirit.
- Romans 8:9: Anyone who does not have the Spirit of Christ does not belong to Him.
- Galatians 4:6: God sent the Spirit of His Son into our hearts, crying, "Abba! Father!"

PRAYER:

Holy Spirit, thank You for dwelling within me and guiding me in truth. Help me to be sensitive to Your leading and to rely on Your presence in every situation. Teach me to walk in obedience and to trust in Your guidance. May my life reflect the peace, joy, and power that come from knowing You. Amen.

PERSONAL REFLECTION:

How can I become more aware of the Holy Spirit's presence in my daily life? What steps can I take to rely on His guidance and strength more fully?

DAY 65: THE POWER OF THE HOLY SPIRIT

Scripture: Acts 1:8 (NASB)

"But you will receive power when the Holy Spirit has come upon you; and you shall be My witnesses both in Jerusalem, and in all Judea and Samaria, and even to the remotest part of the earth."

ANECDOTE:

An artist receives a special set of tools from a master craftsman. These tools are designed to enhance his abilities, allowing him to create beautiful works of art. As he uses them, he discovers a new level of skill and creativity. The tools do not make him an artist, but they empower him to reach his full potential, expressing his vision with greater clarity and impact.

APPLICATION:

The Holy Spirit empowers believers to live out their faith and fulfill God's purpose. Jesus promised His disciples that they would receive power when the Holy Spirit came upon them, enabling them to be His witnesses to the ends of the earth. The power of the Holy Spirit is not limited to certain tasks or people; it is available to all believers, equipping us for ministry, service, and daily living.

The power of the Holy Spirit gives us boldness to share the gospel, strength to overcome sin, wisdom to make godly decisions, and the ability to love others as Christ loves us. It is not about relying on our own abilities but depending on God's power working through us. This power transforms our hearts, renews our minds, and equips us to be effective witnesses of Christ's love and truth. By yielding to the Holy Spirit, we experience His power in every area of our lives, enabling us to live victoriously and purposefully.

FURTHER SCRIPTURE:

- Romans 15:13: May the God of hope fill you with all joy and peace in believing, so that by the power of the Holy Spirit you may abound in hope.
- 1 Corinthians 2:4-5: Paul's message was not with wise words but with a demonstration of the Spirit's power.
- Ephesians 3:16: Paul prays that believers would be strengthened with power through the Spirit in their inner being.

PRAYER:

Holy Spirit, fill me with Your power so that I can be an effective witness for Christ. Strengthen me in my weaknesses, give me boldness to share the gospel, and guide me in truth. Help me to rely on Your power rather than my own abilities. May my life demonstrate Your love, grace, and power to those around me. Amen.

PERSONAL REFLECTION:

How have I experienced the power of the Holy Spirit in my life? In what areas do I need to rely more on His power and less on my own strength?

DAY 66: THE GUIDANCE
OF THE HOLY SPIRIT

Scripture: Romans 8:14 (NASB)
"For all who are being led by the Spirit of God, these are sons of God."

ANECDOTE:

A hiker sets out on a trail he has never walked before. He feels unsure about which direction to take, but he has a guide who knows the path well. By following the guide's lead, the hiker avoids dangerous areas, finds the best viewpoints, and reaches his destination safely. The guide's knowledge and experience make the journey enjoyable and secure.

APPLICATION:

The Holy Spirit is our guide, leading us in the path of righteousness and helping us make wise decisions. Paul tells us in Romans that those who are led by the Spirit of God are children of God. This guidance is one of the privileges of being in a relationship with God. The Holy Spirit knows the way we should go and directs our steps, helping us avoid pitfalls and leading us toward God's purposes.

Being led by the Holy Spirit requires sensitivity and obedience. It means listening for His voice, seeking His direction through prayer, and aligning our actions with God's Word. The Holy Spirit often guides us through Scripture, circumstances, inner promptings, and wise counsel. When we follow His lead, we experience peace, joy, and fulfillment. Trusting in the Holy Spirit's guidance gives us confidence, knowing that God is directing our lives according to His perfect will.

FURTHER SCRIPTURE:

- John 16:13: The Spirit of truth will guide you into all truth.
- Psalm 143:10: Teach me to do Your will, for You are my God; let Your good Spirit lead me on level ground.
- Galatians 5:25: If we live by the Spirit, let us also keep in step with the Spirit.

PRAYER:

Holy Spirit, guide me in all my ways. Help me to hear Your voice clearly and to follow Your lead with trust and obedience. Teach me to seek Your guidance in every decision and to rely on Your wisdom rather than my own understanding. May my life be directed by Your Spirit, reflecting the will of God. Amen.

PERSONAL REFLECTION:

How can I become more attentive to the Holy Spirit's guidance in my daily decisions? What specific areas of my life do I need to surrender to His leading?

DAY 67: THE HOLY SPIRIT AS OUR TEACHER

Scripture: John 14:26 (NASB)
"But the Helper, the Holy Spirit, whom the Father will send in My name, He will teach you all things, and bring to your remembrance all that I said to you."

ANECDOTE:

A student struggles to understand a complex topic in his class. His teacher takes the time to explain the concept patiently, using examples that the student can relate to. As understanding dawns, the student feels grateful for the teacher's guidance. The teacher's ability to make things clear and relevant helps the student learn and apply the knowledge in practical ways.

APPLICATION:

The Holy Spirit is our divine Teacher, sent by the Father to help us understand God's Word and apply it to our lives. Jesus promised that the Holy Spirit would teach us all things and remind us of His teachings. The Holy Spirit illuminates Scripture, revealing its deeper meanings and how it applies to our specific circumstances. He helps us grow in wisdom, knowledge, and understanding, leading us into a deeper relationship with God.

Relying on the Holy Spirit as our Teacher means approaching the Bible with humility and openness, asking for insight and revelation. It involves meditating on God's Word, listening for the Holy Spirit's voice, and being willing to learn and be corrected. As we grow in our understanding of Scripture, we become better equipped to live according to God's will and to share His truth with others. The Holy Spirit's teaching is a continuous process that guides us through life's challenges and strengthens our faith.

FURTHER SCRIPTURE:

- 1 Corinthians 2:13: We speak not in words taught by human wisdom but in words taught by the Spirit, explaining spiritual realities.
- Psalm 119:18: Open my eyes, that I may behold wonderful things from Your law.
- 1 John 2:27: The anointing you received from Him remains in you, and His anointing teaches you about all things.

PRAYER:

Holy Spirit, thank You for being my Teacher and guiding me into all truth. Open my mind and heart to understand Your Word more deeply. Help me to be attentive to Your teaching and to apply what I learn in my daily life. May Your wisdom fill me and lead me closer to God. Amen.

PERSONAL REFLECTION:

How can I be more intentional about seeking the Holy Spirit's teaching as I read the Bible? What steps can I take to allow His truth to shape my thoughts, actions, and decisions?

DAY 68: THE COMFORT OF THE HOLY SPIRIT

Scripture: John 14:16 (NASB)

"I will ask the Father, and He will give you another Helper, that He may be with you forever."

ANECDOTE:

A friend sits with another who has just received difficult news. Without saying much, the friend's presence brings comfort and reassurance. Knowing that someone is there, offering a listening ear and compassionate support, makes the burden easier to bear. The friend's comforting presence is a source of strength during a challenging time.

APPLICATION:

The Holy Spirit is not only our Teacher and Guide; He is also our Comforter. Jesus promised to send another Helper, the Holy Spirit, to be with us forever. The Holy Spirit brings peace, comfort, and encouragement, especially in times of sorrow, fear, or uncertainty. His presence assures us that we are not alone, no matter what we face.

The Holy Spirit's comfort comes through His presence within us, reminding us of God's love, faithfulness, and promises. He helps us in our weaknesses, interceding for us with groanings too deep for words (Romans 8:26). When we are overwhelmed, the Holy Spirit provides the strength we need to endure and the peace that surpasses understanding. Turning to the Holy Spirit for comfort involves prayer, resting in God's presence, and trusting in His care. As we lean on the Holy Spirit, we find solace and hope, knowing that He is with us, guiding us through every trial.

FURTHER SCRIPTURE:

- 2 Corinthians 1:3-4: God comforts us in all our troubles so that we can comfort others.
- Psalm 23:4: Even though I walk through the valley of the shadow of death, I will fear no evil, for You are with me.
- Romans 15:13: May the God of hope fill you with all joy and peace in believing.

PRAYER:

Holy Spirit, thank You for being my Comforter. In times of trouble, fear, or sorrow, remind me of Your presence and the peace that comes from trusting in You. Fill my heart with Your comfort, and give me the strength to face each Day with hope. May I be a source of comfort to others, sharing the love and encouragement that You have given me. Amen.

PERSONAL REFLECTION:

How have I experienced the Holy Spirit's comfort in my life? How can I seek His presence more intentionally in times of difficulty or uncertainty?

DAY 69: THE TRANSFORMING POWER OF THE HOLY SPIRIT

Scripture: 2 Corinthians 3:18 (NASB)

"But we all, with unveiled face, beholding as in a mirror the glory of the Lord, are being transformed into the same image from glory to glory, just as from the Lord, the Spirit."

ANECDOTE:

A sculptor works patiently on a block of marble, chipping away at imperfections, refining details, and shaping it into a masterpiece. What started as a rough stone becomes a beautiful work of art, reflecting the sculptor's vision and skill. The transformation process takes time and care, but the end result is worth the effort.

APPLICATION:

The Holy Spirit plays a crucial role in transforming our lives to reflect the image of Christ. Paul writes in 2 Corinthians that as we behold the glory of the Lord, we are being transformed into His image. This transformation is a continuous process, moving from one level of glory to another, by the power of the Holy Spirit. It involves changing our thoughts, attitudes, behaviors, and desires to align with God's will.

Transformation by the Holy Spirit requires our cooperation. It involves spending time in God's presence, reading His Word, praying, and yielding to the Holy Spirit's work in our lives. The Holy Spirit convicts us of sin, leads us to repentance, and empowers us to live righteously. As we surrender to His leading, we experience spiritual growth and become more like Jesus. The transforming power of the Holy Spirit enables us to overcome sinful habits, develop godly character, and bear the fruit of the Spirit, reflecting God's love and holiness to the world.

FURTHER SCRIPTURE:

- Romans 12:2: Be transformed by the renewing of your mind.
- Philippians 1:6: He who began a good work in you will bring it to completion.
- Galatians 5:22-23: The fruit of the Spirit is love, joy, peace, patience, kindness, goodness, faithfulness, gentleness, and self-control.

PRAYER:

Holy Spirit, I invite You to transform my life. Change my heart, mind, and actions to reflect the image of Christ. Help me to let go of anything that hinders Your work in me and to embrace the changes You are making. May I grow in love, holiness, and righteousness, becoming more like Jesus each Day. Thank You for Your patience and power in transforming me. Amen.

PERSONAL REFLECTION:

What areas of my life need transformation by the Holy Spirit? How can I cooperate more fully with His work to become more like Christ?

DAY 70: LIVING A SPIRIT-FILLED LIFE

Scripture: Galatians 5:16 (NASB)
"But I say, walk by the Spirit, and you will
not carry out the desire of the flesh."

ANECDOTE:

A sailboat relies on the wind to move across the water. The sailor adjusts the sails to catch the wind, guiding the boat in the desired direction. Without the wind, the boat would drift aimlessly or remain still. But with the wind's power, the boat can navigate the open sea with purpose and speed.

APPLICATION:

Living a Spirit-filled life means walking by the Spirit, allowing His presence and power to guide our actions, decisions, and attitudes. Paul encourages believers to walk by the Spirit to avoid fulfilling the desires of the flesh. The flesh represents our sinful nature, which is contrary to God's will. In contrast, walking by the Spirit leads to a life characterized by righteousness, peace, and joy.

Living a Spirit-filled life requires intentionality and dependence on the Holy Spirit. It means daily seeking God's presence, submitting to His will, and being sensitive to His leading. This involves regular prayer, studying Scripture, and being open to the Holy Spirit's conviction and guidance. A Spirit-filled life is marked by the fruit of the Spirit, demonstrating love, patience, kindness, and self-control. As we walk by the Spirit, we experience freedom from sin's power and the ability to live victoriously in Christ.

FURTHER SCRIPTURE:

- Ephesians 5:18: Do not get drunk with wine, for that is debauchery, but be filled with the Spirit.
- Romans 8:5: Those who live according to the Spirit set their minds on the things of the Spirit.
- Colossians 3:16: Let the word of Christ dwell in you richly, teaching and admonishing one another in all wisdom.

PRAYER:

Holy Spirit, fill me with Your presence each Day. Help me to walk by the Spirit, choosing Your way over my own desires. Guide my thoughts, actions, and words, so that they reflect Your love and truth. Empower me to live a life that honors God, bearing the fruit of the Spirit and shining as a light in the world. Amen.

PERSONAL REFLECTION:

What does it mean for me to walk by the Spirit in my daily life? How can I cultivate a deeper dependence on the Holy Spirit's guidance and power?

FIRMING UP YOUR FAITH
THE HOLY SPIRIT

- Reflect on the promise and power of the Holy Spirit in your life. How does it give you strength?

- How does the guidance of the Holy Spirit influence your decisions and daily actions?

- What does it mean for the Holy Spirit to be your Teacher, and how can you rely on Him more?

- In what ways has the Spirit's comfort been evident in your life?

- How can you pursue a Spirit-filled life that reflects transformation?

WEEK 11
THE RETURN OF CHRIST

DAY 71: THE PROMISE OF CHRIST'S RETURN

Scripture: John 14:3 (NASB)
"If I go and prepare a place for you, I will come again and receive you to Myself, that where I am, there you may be also."

ANECDOTE:

A parent promises their child that after a long Day of work, they will return home to spend time together. The child waits eagerly, looking out the window, excitedly anticipating the moment they see their parent's car in the driveway. This promise gives the child hope and comfort, knowing that their parent will keep their word and be with them soon.

APPLICATION:

Jesus promised His disciples that He would return to take them to be with Him. This promise is not just for the disciples of Jesus' time but for all believers. The promise of Christ's return gives us hope, comfort, and encouragement in our daily lives. Knowing that Jesus is preparing a place for us and will come again to take us to be with Him reassures us of His love and faithfulness.

Christ's return reminds us that this world is not our final home; we have a heavenly home prepared by Jesus Himself. This truth motivates us to live with a heavenly perspective, focusing on things that have eternal value. It also encourages us to persevere through trials, knowing that our struggles are temporary compared to the eternal joy that awaits us. Believing in the promise of Christ's return inspires us to live faithfully, sharing the hope of Jesus with others and preparing our hearts to meet Him.

FURTHER SCRIPTURE:

- Acts 1:11: The angels told the disciples that Jesus would return in the same way they saw Him go into heaven.
- 1 Thessalonians 4:16-17: The Lord Himself will descend from heaven, and we will be caught up together with Him.
- Revelation 22:12: Jesus says, "Behold, I am coming soon, bringing my recompense with me."

PRAYER:

Lord Jesus, thank You for the promise of Your return. Help me to live each Day with anticipation and hope, knowing that You are coming back to take me to be with You. Strengthen my faith and keep my heart focused on eternal things. May I be ready for Your return, living a life that honors You. Amen.

PERSONAL REFLECTION:

How does the promise of Christ's return impact my daily life? What steps can I take to live with a greater sense of anticipation and readiness for His coming?

DAY 72: THE SIGNS OF HIS COMING

Scripture: Matthew 24:30 (NASB)
"And then the sign of the Son of Man will ap-
pear in the sky, and then all the tribes of the earth will
mourn, and they will see the Son of Man coming on
the clouds of the sky with power and great glory."

ANECDOTE:

A traveler watches the sky as storm clouds begin to gather on the horizon. The darkening clouds, distant thunder, and increasing wind all signal that a storm is approaching. By recognizing these signs, the traveler knows to seek shelter and prepare for the coming storm. Awareness of the signs allows the traveler to respond appropriately.

APPLICATION:

Jesus spoke of various signs that would precede His return, such as wars, famines, earthquakes, and persecution. These signs are not meant to scare us but to prepare us. They remind us to stay alert and vigilant, keeping our eyes fixed on Jesus. The signs of His coming also remind us of the urgency of sharing the gospel, as we do not know the exact Day or hour of His return.

Recognizing the signs of Jesus' return helps us to live with a sense of urgency and purpose. Instead of becoming fearful or anxious, we are called to be watchful and prayerful, trusting in God's sovereignty. The signs are a call to action, motivating us to live holy and godly lives, to love others, and to be ready for Jesus' return. By understanding the signs, we remain faithful and focused, confident that God's plan is unfolding as He has promised.

FURTHER SCRIPTURE:

- Matthew 24:6-8: Jesus describes wars, famines, and earthquakes as the beginning of birth pains.
- Luke 21:28: Jesus tells us to stand up and lift our heads because our redemption is drawing near.
- 2 Timothy 3:1-5: Paul describes the last days as difficult times, marked by sin and godlessness.

PRAYER:

Heavenly Father, help me to recognize the signs of Your Son's coming and to live with a heart of readiness. Teach me to be watchful, prayerful, and faithful, trusting in Your timing and plan. May I live each Day with a sense of purpose and urgency, sharing the hope of Jesus with others and preparing my heart for His return. Amen.

PERSONAL REFLECTION:

What are some signs of Jesus' return that I see in the world toDay? How can I respond with faith and readiness to these signs, living a life that honors God?

DAY 73: THE HOPE OF RESURRECTION

Scripture: 1 Corinthians 15:52 (NASB)
"In a moment, in the twinkling of an eye, at the last trumpet; for the trumpet will sound, and the dead will be raised imperishable, and we will be changed."

ANECDOTE:

A gardener plants a seed in the soil, knowing that it will one Day sprout, grow, and bloom into a beautiful flower. Though the seed appears lifeless, it holds the promise of new life within. The gardener's hope is not in the seed itself but in the process of growth and transformation that will bring forth new life.

APPLICATION:

The resurrection of the dead is a central hope of the Christian faith. Paul speaks of the Day when the last trumpet will sound, and the dead will be raised imperishable, and those who are alive will be changed. This hope of resurrection is rooted in the resurrection of Jesus Christ, who conquered death and gave us the promise of eternal life. The resurrection assures us that death is not the end; it is a doorway to eternal life with God.

The hope of resurrection gives us comfort in the face of loss, knowing that we will be reunited with our loved ones who have died in Christ. It also gives us courage to face trials, suffering, and even death, knowing that our bodies will be transformed, and we will live forever with God. The promise of resurrection motivates us to live for Christ, laying aside temporary concerns and focusing on what is eternal. This hope is not wishful thinking; it is a confident expectation based on the truth of God's Word.

FURTHER SCRIPTURE:

- John 11:25-26: Jesus said, "I am the resurrection and the life. He who believes in Me will live, even though he dies."
- 1 Thessalonians 4:16-17: The dead in Christ will rise first, and we who are alive will be caught up together with them.
- Philippians 3:20-21: We eagerly await a Savior, the Lord Jesus Christ, who will transform our lowly bodies.

PRAYER:

Lord, thank You for the hope of resurrection and eternal life through Jesus Christ. Help me to live with this hope in my heart, knowing that death is not the end but the beginning of eternal joy with You. Strengthen my faith and fill me with the assurance of Your promises. May I live each Day with the hope of resurrection, bringing comfort and encouragement to others. Amen.

PERSONAL REFLECTION:

How does the hope of resurrection impact my view of life and death? In what ways can I encourage others with the hope of eternal life in Christ?

DAY 74: LIVING IN READINESS FOR CHRIST'S RETURN

Scripture: Matthew 24:44 (NASB)
"For this reason you also must be ready; for the Son of Man is coming at an hour when you do not think He will."

ANECDOTE:

A fire drill is conducted in a school to prepare students for an emergency. When the alarm sounds, the students know to leave their classrooms and follow their teachers to safety. Practicing the drill helps them to be ready and calm in case of a real emergency, knowing exactly what to do without hesitation.

APPLICATION:

Jesus emphasized the importance of being ready for His return, as it will come at an unexpected time. Living in readiness means being spiritually prepared, staying alert, and not becoming complacent. It involves living a life that honors God, repenting of sin, and being faithful in our walk with Christ. Readiness is not about predicting dates or being fearful; it is about living faithfully and expectantly each Day.

To live in readiness for Christ's return, we need to cultivate a heart of watchfulness and prayer. This includes being diligent in our relationship with God, growing in our faith, and staying connected with other believers. It also means serving others, sharing the gospel, and using our gifts for God's glory. Readiness is an active state, where we are engaged in God's work and looking forward to the day when we will see Jesus face to face. Living in readiness brings peace and joy, knowing that we are prepared to meet our Savior.

FURTHER SCRIPTURE:

- Mark 13:33: Be on guard, keep awake, for you do not know when the time will come.
- Luke 12:35-36: Be dressed and ready for service, with your lamps burning, like men waiting for their master to return.
- 1 Peter 4:7: The end of all things is near; therefore, be clear-minded and self-controlled so that you can pray.

PRAYER:

Lord Jesus, help me to live each Day in readiness for Your return. Keep my heart watchful and my spirit alert, so that I am prepared to meet You. Teach me to live faithfully, serving others and sharing Your love. May I not become complacent but stay focused on You, looking forward to the Day of Your coming. Amen.

PERSONAL REFLECTION:

What does it mean to be ready for Christ's return? How can I cultivate a heart of readiness and live each Day with anticipation of Jesus' coming?

DAY 75: ENCOURAGING ONE ANOTHER WITH THE HOPE OF HIS RETURN

Scripture: 1 Thessalonians 4:18 (NASB)
"Therefore comfort one another with these words."

ANECDOTE:

A family waits for a loved one to return home after a long trip. Each Day, they talk about the reunion, sharing memories and expressing their excitement. Their conversations are filled with joy and hope, knowing that their loved one's return is near. This shared anticipation strengthens their bond and brings comfort, even in the waiting.

APPLICATION:

The return of Christ is a source of great hope and comfort for believers. Paul encourages the Thessalonians to comfort one another with the promise of Christ's return and the resurrection of the dead. This hope brings peace and assurance, reminding us that our future is secure in Christ. It also encourages us to remain faithful, knowing that Jesus will return to set all things right.

As believers, we are called to encourage one another with the hope of Christ's return. This involves sharing the promises of Scripture, praying for one another, and reminding each other of God's faithfulness. In times of sorrow, fear, or uncertainty, the hope of Jesus' return brings comfort and strength. Encouraging one another with this hope helps us to stay focused on God's promises, supporting each other as we wait for the day when we will be with Him forever.

FURTHER SCRIPTURE:

- Hebrews 10:25: Encourage one another, and all the more as you see the Day approaching.
- Titus 2:13: We wait for the blessed hope—the appearing of the glory of our great God and Savior, Jesus Christ.
- Romans 15:13: May the God of hope fill you with all joy and peace as you trust in Him.

PRAYER:

Heavenly Father, thank You for the hope of Christ's return and the comfort it brings. Help me to encourage others with this hope, sharing the promises of Your Word and supporting one another in faith. Fill my heart with joy and anticipation, knowing that Jesus is coming soon. May my life be a reflection of the hope I have in You. Amen.

PERSONAL REFLECTION:

How can I encourage others with the hope of Christ's return? In what ways can I share the comfort and joy of this promise with those around me?

DAY 76: THE FINAL JUDGMENT

Scripture: Revelation 20:12 (NASB)
"And I saw the dead, the great and the small, standing before the throne, and books were opened; and another book was opened, which is the book of life; and the dead were judged from the things which were written in the books, according to their deeds."

ANECDOTE:

A student takes a final exam after a semester of study. The exam determines the outcome of their efforts, testing their knowledge and understanding. The student knows that preparation and hard work will be evaluated, and the result will reflect their commitment to learning. The exam serves as a reminder of the importance of diligence and responsibility.

APPLICATION:

The Bible speaks of a final judgment when all people will stand before God's throne and be judged according to their deeds. This judgment will reveal the righteousness of God and the justice of His decisions. For believers the final judgment is not a source of fear but of hope, knowing that our salvation is secure in Christ and our names are written in the book of life.

The knowledge of the final judgment encourages us to live with integrity, accountability, and a heart that seeks to please God. It reminds us that our actions, choices, and attitudes matter and that we are called to live in a way that honors God. The final judgment also motivates us to share the gospel with others, knowing that everyone will stand before God one day. By living with an eternal perspective, we focus on what truly matters and invest our lives in things that have lasting value.

FURTHER SCRIPTURE:

- Matthew 25:31-32: The Son of Man will separate the people as a shepherd separates the sheep from the goats.
- 2 Corinthians 5:10: We must all appear before the judgment seat of Christ.
- Hebrews 9:27: It is appointed for man to die once, and after that comes judgment.

PRAYER:

Lord, help me to live with the awareness of the final judgment, seeking to honor You in all that I do. Thank You for the assurance of salvation through Jesus Christ and for the promise of eternal life. Guide my actions, words, and thoughts to reflect Your love and holiness. May my life bring glory to Your name, and may I be faithful in sharing the hope of the gospel with others. Amen.

PERSONAL REFLECTION:

How does the knowledge of the final judgment impact my choices and actions? What can I do to live with a greater sense of responsibility and commitment to God's will?

DAY 77: THE NEW HEAVEN AND NEW EARTH

Scripture: Revelation 21:1 (NASB)
"Then I saw a new heaven and a new earth; for the first heaven and the first earth passed away, and there is no longer any sea."

ANECDOTE:

A family moves into a newly built home, leaving behind their old, worn-out house. The new home is everything they hoped for: spacious, beautiful, and filled with light. The excitement of new beginnings and the joy of a fresh start fill their hearts as they settle into their new surroundings, knowing that this place is where they will create lasting memories together.

APPLICATION:

The Bible speaks of a new heaven and a new earth, where God will dwell with His people, and there will be no more pain, sorrow, or death. This promise of a renewed creation gives us hope for the future, knowing that God is making all things new. The new heaven and new earth are a place of eternal joy, peace, and fellowship with God.

The hope of a new heaven and new earth encourages us to look beyond our present circumstances and to focus on the eternal promises of God. It reminds us that the struggles and difficulties of this world are temporary compared to the glory that awaits us. This hope motivates us to persevere in faith, knowing that God's plan is unfolding and that He will fulfill His promises. As we look forward to the new heaven and new earth, we are inspired to live holy and godly lives, preparing our hearts for the day when we will dwell with God forever.

FURTHER SCRIPTURE:

- 2 Peter 3:13: According to His promise, we are looking for new heavens and a new earth, in which righteousness dwells.
- Isaiah 65:17: God promises to create new heavens and a new earth, and the former things will not be remembered.
- Revelation 21:4: God will wipe away every tear, and there will be no more death, mourning, crying, or pain.

PRAYER:

Heavenly Father, thank You for the promise of a new heaven and a new earth. Fill my heart with hope and joy as I look forward to the Day when I will dwell with You forever. Help me to live with an eternal perspective, focusing on Your promises and seeking to honor You in all that I do. May my life be a reflection of the hope I have in You. Amen.

PERSONAL REFLECTION:

How does the promise of a new heaven and new earth give me hope? In what ways can I live with a greater sense of anticipation and readiness for God's eternal kingdom?

FIRMING UP YOUR FAITH
THE RETURN OF CHRIST

- How does the promise of Christ's return give you hope and shape your perspective?

- What are some signs of His coming that encourage you to stay vigilant?

- How can you live in readiness for Christ's return each day?

- In what ways can you encourage others with the hope of Christ's return?

- How does the knowledge of the final judgment impact your commitment to follow Jesus?

WEEK 12
THE CHRISTIAN'S HOPE

DAY 78: THE LIVING HOPE
THROUGH JESUS CHRIST

DAY 79: THE ASSURANCE
OF ETERNAL LIFE

DAY 80: THE JOY OF BEING
IN GOD'S PRESENCE

DAY 81: THE REALITY OF HEAVEN

DAY 82: LIVING WITH AN
ETERNAL PERSPECTIVE

DAY 83: THE REWARD OF FAITHFULNESS

DAY 84: THE CROWN OF LIFE

DAY 78: THE LIVING HOPE THROUGH JESUS CHRIST

Scripture: 1 Peter 1:3 (NASB)

"Blessed be the God and Father of our Lord Jesus Christ, who according to His great mercy has caused us to be born again to a living hope through the resurrection of Jesus Christ from the dead."

ANECDOTE:

A sailor lost at sea for Days spots a rescue boat on the horizon. Hope surges through him as he sees the boat approaching, knowing that his ordeal is almost over. The sight of the boat fills him with renewed energy and determination to hold on, knowing that rescue is near and his life will be saved.

APPLICATION:

As believers, we have a living hope through Jesus Christ—a hope that is alive and active, rooted in the resurrection of Christ from the dead. This living hope is not just a wishful thought or a vague expectation; it is a confident assurance based on the truth of Jesus' victory over sin and death. Through His resurrection, we are born again into a new life, filled with hope that sustains us in all circumstances.

This living hope transforms our outlook on life. It gives us strength to endure trials, knowing that our present sufferings are not worth comparing with the glory that will be revealed in us (Romans 8:18). It provides peace in times of uncertainty, assurance in the face of death, and joy in the promise of eternal life. Living with this hope means focusing on Jesus, trusting in His promises, and sharing the hope we have with others. Our living hope in Christ motivates us to live faithfully, knowing that our future is secure in Him.

FURTHER SCRIPTURE:

- Titus 2:13: We wait for the blessed hope—the appearing of the glory of our great God and Savior, Jesus Christ.
- Colossians 1:27: Christ in you, the hope of glory.
- Romans 5:5: Hope does not disappoint, because the love of God has been poured out within our hearts through the Holy Spirit.

PRAYER:

Lord, thank You for the living hope I have through Jesus Christ. Help me to hold onto this hope in every circumstance, trusting in Your promises and the assurance of eternal life. Fill my heart with joy and peace, knowing that my hope is secure in You. May I share this hope with others, offering encouragement and pointing them to the source of true hope. Amen.

PERSONAL REFLECTION:

How does the living hope of Jesus Christ impact my daily life? In what ways can I share this hope with those around me, offering encouragement and pointing them to Christ?

DAY 79: THE ASSURANCE OF ETERNAL LIFE

Scripture: 1 John 5:11-12 (NASB)
"And the testimony is this, that God has given us eternal life,
and this life is in His Son. He who has the Son has the life; he
who does not have the Son of God does not have the life."

ANECDOTE:

A young student receives a scholarship to attend a prestigious university. The scholarship guarantees his education, providing all the resources he needs to succeed. The assurance of this scholarship gives him confidence and peace of mind, knowing that his future is secure and his path is set.

APPLICATION:

The assurance of eternal life is one of the greatest gifts we receive through faith in Jesus Christ. John reminds us that God has given us eternal life, and this life is found in His Son. Eternal life is not just a future promise; it is a present reality for those who believe in Jesus. It begins the moment we accept Christ as our Savior and continues forever in His presence.

This assurance brings peace, knowing that nothing can separate us from the love of God (Romans 8:38-39). It gives us confidence in our salvation, knowing that our eternal destiny is secure in Christ. The assurance of eternal life frees us from the fear of death and empowers us to live boldly for God's glory. By focusing on our eternal inheritance, we are motivated to live a life that honors God, sharing His love and truth with others. The assurance of eternal life fills us with joy, gratitude, and a sense of purpose.

FURTHER SCRIPTURE:

- John 10:28: Jesus says, "I give them eternal life, and they shall never perish; no one can snatch them out of My hand."
- Romans 6:23: The gift of God is eternal life in Christ Jesus our Lord.
- John 3:36: Whoever believes in the Son has eternal life.

PRAYER:

Heavenly Father, thank You for the gift of eternal life through Your Son, Jesus Christ. Help me to live each Day with the assurance of this promise, free from fear and filled with confidence in Your love. May my life reflect the joy and peace that come from knowing I am secure in You. Teach me to share this assurance with others, leading them to the hope found in Christ. Amen.

PERSONAL REFLECTION:

How does the assurance of eternal life influence my perspective on life and death? In what ways can I live with greater confidence and joy, knowing that my eternal future is secure in Christ?

DAY 80: THE JOY OF BEING IN GOD'S PRESENCE

Scripture: Psalm 16:11 (NASB)
"You will make known to me the path of life; in Your presence is fullness of joy; in Your right hand there are pleasures forever."

ANECDOTE:

A child looks forward to the end of the school Day, knowing that their parent will be waiting to take them home. The joy of being in their parent's presence, talking about the Day, and spending time together is the highlight of the child's Day. The relationship they share brings a sense of happiness, security, and love that nothing else can match.

APPLICATION:

Being in God's presence brings fullness of joy, peace, and contentment. The psalmist declares that in God's presence there is fullness of joy and eternal pleasures. This joy is not dependent on circumstances but is found in a deep, personal relationship with God. The joy of being in God's presence comes from knowing that He loves us, cares for us, and is with us always.

Spending time in God's presence through prayer, worship, and meditating on His Word refreshes our spirit and renews our strength. It reminds us of God's faithfulness, goodness, and the eternal life we have in Him. As we experience the joy of God's presence, we are filled with hope and peace that transcends our understanding. This joy sustains us through trials, comforts us in sorrow, and motivates us to live a life of praise and gratitude. The joy of being in God's presence is a foretaste of the eternal joy we will experience in heaven.

FURTHER SCRIPTURE:

- Nehemiah 8:10: The joy of the Lord is your strength.
- Philippians 4:4: Rejoice in the Lord always; again I will say, rejoice!
- Psalm 27:4: One thing I ask of the Lord, this is what I seek: that I may dwell in the house of the Lord all the days of my life.

PRAYER:

Lord, thank You for the joy that comes from being in Your presence. Help me to seek You daily, finding strength, peace, and joy in my relationship with You. Fill my heart with the fullness of joy that only You can provide. May my life be a reflection of Your joy, drawing others to experience Your love and presence. Amen.

PERSONAL REFLECTION:

How can I spend more time in God's presence and experience the joy He offers? In what ways can I share the joy of being in God's presence with others?

DAY 81: THE REALITY OF HEAVEN

Scripture: Revelation 21:4 (NASB)
"And He will wipe away every tear from their eyes; and there will no longer be any death; there will no longer be any mourning, or crying, or pain; the first things have passed away."

ANECDOTE:

A traveler reaches the end of a long, difficult journey and arrives at a beautiful, peaceful destination. The challenges and hardships of the journey fade away in the face of the beauty and rest that surround him. The joy of reaching this destination fills his heart, knowing that all the struggles were worth it to arrive at this place of peace and comfort.

APPLICATION:

Heaven is a real place, a place of eternal joy, peace, and the presence of God. In heaven, there will be no more pain, sorrow, or death. God Himself will wipe away every tear from our eyes, and we will experience the fullness of His love and glory. The reality of heaven gives us hope, knowing that the trials and suffering of this life are temporary compared to the eternal joy that awaits us.

Thinking about heaven helps us to live with an eternal perspective, focusing on what truly matters. It reminds us to invest our lives in things that have lasting value and to seek God's kingdom above all else. The reality of heaven motivates us to share the gospel, desiring that others also experience the joy of eternal life with God. As we look forward to heaven, we find comfort in knowing that our future is secure, and we will dwell with God forever in a place of perfect peace and joy.

FURTHER SCRIPTURE:

- John 14:2-3: Jesus says, "In My Father's house are many rooms. I am going there to prepare a place for you."
- Philippians 3:20: Our citizenship is in heaven, and we eagerly await a Savior from there.
- Hebrews 11:16: They desire a better country, that is, a heavenly one.

PRAYER:

Heavenly Father, thank You for the promise of heaven and the hope it brings. Help me to live with an eternal perspective, focusing on Your promises and the joy of being with You forever. Strengthen my faith and comfort my heart with the reality of heaven. May my life reflect the hope of eternity, sharing Your love and truth with others. Amen.

PERSONAL REFLECTION:

How does the reality of heaven shape my view of life and eternity? In what ways can I live with a greater focus on God's kingdom and the hope of heaven?

DAY 82: LIVING WITH AN ETERNAL PERSPECTIVE

Scripture: 2 Corinthians 4:18 (NASB)
"So we fix our eyes not on what is seen, but on what is unseen, since what is seen is temporary, but what is unseen is eternal."

ANECDOTE:

A mountain climber focuses on the peak of the mountain as he climbs. The path is steep and challenging, but he keeps his eyes on the summit, knowing that reaching the top is worth the effort. His focus on the goal gives him the determination to continue climbing, despite the obstacles along the way.

APPLICATION:

Living with an eternal perspective means focusing on what is unseen and eternal rather than what is temporary and visible. Paul encourages believers to fix their eyes on eternal things, recognizing that the struggles and challenges of this life are momentary compared to the eternal glory that awaits us. An eternal perspective helps us prioritize our lives, making decisions that align with God's will and purpose.

By focusing on eternity we are less likely to be swayed by the fleeting pleasures and pressures of this world. We find peace and joy in knowing that our ultimate home is with God and that He is preparing a place for us. Living with an eternal perspective also motivates us to invest our time, talents, and resources in God's kingdom, sharing the gospel, serving others, and making a lasting impact. As we keep our eyes on eternity, we are strengthened to persevere, encouraged to live faithfully, and inspired to fulfill God's calling for our lives.

FURTHER SCRIPTURE:

- Colossians 3:2: Set your minds on things above, not on earthly things.
- Hebrews 12:2: Fixing our eyes on Jesus, the pioneer and perfecter of our faith.
- Matthew 6:19-20: Do not store up for yourselves treasures on earth but store up treasures in heaven.

PRAYER:

Lord, help me to live with an eternal perspective, focusing on what is unseen and lasting. Teach me to prioritize my life according to Your will, investing in things that have eternal value. Give me the strength to persevere through challenges, knowing that my future is secure in You. May my life be a reflection of my hope in eternity, bringing glory to Your name. Amen.

PERSONAL REFLECTION:

How can I cultivate an eternal perspective in my daily life? What changes can I make to focus more on God's kingdom and less on temporary concerns?

DAY 83: THE REWARD
OF FAITHFULNESS

Scripture: Matthew 25:21 (NASB)

"His master said to him, 'Well done, good and faithful servant. You were faithful with a few things; I will put you in charge of many things; enter into the joy of your master.'"

ANECDOTE:

An employee works diligently, going above and beyond in his tasks. His dedication and commitment do not go unnoticed. At the end of the year, he is recognized by his employer, receiving a promotion and a heartfelt commendation for his hard work. The reward for his faithfulness brings him joy and satisfaction, knowing that his efforts were appreciated and valued.

APPLICATION:

God values faithfulness, and He promises to reward those who are faithful to Him. Jesus' parable of the talents illustrates the importance of being faithful stewards of what God has entrusted to us. Faithfulness is not about having the most or doing the most; it is about using what we have been given to serve God and others. The reward of faithfulness is not just material blessings; it is the joy of hearing God say, "Well done, good and faithful servant."

Being faithful involves obedience, perseverance, and a heart that seeks to honor God in all things. It means serving with humility, loving others, and sharing the gospel, regardless of the results. God's reward for faithfulness includes the joy of His presence, the satisfaction of fulfilling His purpose, and the promise of eternal life. Living faithfully is a daily commitment, trusting that God sees our efforts and will honor our faithfulness. As we remain faithful, we bring glory to God and experience the joy of serving Him.

FURTHER SCRIPTURE:

- Hebrews 11:6: Without faith, it is impossible to please God, for whoever would draw near to God must believe that He exists and rewards those who seek Him.
- Revelation 2:10: Be faithful, even to the point of death, and I will give you the crown of life.
- 1 Corinthians 4:2: It is required of stewards that they be found faithful.

PRAYER:

Heavenly Father, help me to be a faithful servant, using the gifts and opportunities You have given me to serve You and others. Teach me to live with integrity, perseverance, and a heart that seeks to honor You in all things. May my life bring glory to Your name, and may I hear the words, "Well done, good and faithful servant." Thank You for Your promise to reward faithfulness. Amen.

PERSONAL REFLECTION:

How can I be more faithful in my relationship with God and in serving others? What specific actions can I take to demonstrate faithfulness in my daily life?

DAY 84: THE CROWN OF LIFE

Scripture: James 1:12 (NASB)
*"Blessed is a man who perseveres under trial; for once
he has been approved, he will receive the crown of life
which the Lord has promised to those who love Him."*

ANECDOTE:

A marathon runner pushes through pain and exhaustion to reach the finish line. Despite the challenges, the runner keeps going, motivated by the vision of crossing the finish line and receiving the medal that signifies victory. The reward is not just a piece of metal but the accomplishment of completing the race and the recognition of his perseverance and dedication.

APPLICATION:

The crown of life is a reward promised to those who persevere in their faith through trials and tribulations. James encourages believers to endure under trial, knowing that God will reward their faithfulness. The crown of life is not just a symbol of eternal life but a recognition of the love and devotion we have shown to God, even in the face of adversity.

Persevering under trial requires faith, trust, and a deep love for God. It means holding on to His promises, seeking His strength, and relying on His grace. The trials we face in this life are temporary, but the reward of the crown of life is eternal. Knowing that God sees our struggles and will honor our perseverance gives us the courage to continue, no matter the obstacles. The crown of life is a reminder that our faith is not in vain and that God's promises are true.

FURTHER SCRIPTURE:

- Revelation 2:10: Be faithful unto death, and I will give you the crown of life.
- 2 Timothy 4:8: There is laid up for me the crown of righteousness, which the Lord will award to me on that day.
- 1 Peter 5:4: When the Chief Shepherd appears, you will receive the unfading crown of glory.

PRAYER:

Lord, thank You for the promise of the crown of life for those who persevere in faith. Help me to endure under trial, trusting in Your strength and holding on to Your promises. Fill my heart with love for You, and give me the courage to remain faithful, no matter what challenges I face. May I run the race with perseverance, keeping my eyes on Jesus, the author and finisher of my faith. Amen.

PERSONAL REFLECTION:

What trials am I currently facing, and how can I persevere with faith and trust in God? How does the promise of the crown of life encourage me to remain faithful and devoted to God?

FIRMING UP YOUR FAITH
DISCIPLESHIP AND GROWTH

- Reflect on the call to discipleship. What does it mean for you personally?

- How does abiding in Christ affect your growth and spiritual maturity?

- What are the costs of discipleship, and how can you embrace them joyfully?

- Who can you find mentorship or accountability in your faith journey?

- What areas of your life show evidence of becoming more like Christ?

WEEK 13 THE SEVEN CHURCHES OF REVELATION

Day 85: The Church of Ephesus – Remember Your First Love

Day 86: The Church of Smyrna – Faithful Unto Death

Day 87: The Church of Pergamum – Holding Fast to the Truth

Day 88: The Church of Thyatira – Growing in Love and Service

Day 89: The Church of Sardis – Wake Up and Strengthen What Remains

Day 90: The Church of Philadelphia – An Open Door

Day 91: The Church of Laodicea – Lukewarm No More

DAY 85: THE CHURCH OF EPHESUS – REMEMBER YOUR FIRST LOVE

Scripture: Revelation 2:4-5 (NASB)
*"But I have this against you, that you have left your first love.
Therefore remember from where you have fallen, and repent and
do the deeds you did at first; or else I am coming to you and will
remove your lampstand out of its place—unless you repent."*

ANECDOTE:

A couple who had been married for many years began to feel distant from each other. The busyness of life and routine had caused them to drift apart. One Day, they decided to take a trip to the place where they first met and fell in love. As they reminisced about their early Days together, they were reminded of the love that brought them together and rekindled their commitment to each other.

APPLICATION:

The church in Ephesus was commended for their hard work, perseverance, and discernment, but they had lost their first love for Christ. Jesus called them to remember, repent, and return to the love they had at first. This message is a reminder that our relationship with Jesus is about love, not just duty. It's easy to get caught up in the busyness of serving God and forget the joy of being in His presence.

Returning to our first love means rekindling our passion for Christ, prioritizing our relationship with Him, and worshiping with a heart full of love. It involves spending time in prayer, reading God's Word, and remembering the joy of our salvation. When our love for Christ is renewed, it overflows into our service, making it a joyful expression of our devotion to Him. Let's remember our first love and keep our hearts focused on Jesus.

FURTHER SCRIPTURE:

- Matthew 22:37-38: Love the Lord your God with all your heart, soul, and mind.
- Jeremiah 2:2: God remembers the devotion of Israel's youth, their love as a bride.
- Psalm 51:12: Restore to me the joy of Your salvation.

PRAYER:

Lord Jesus, help me to remember my first love for You. Forgive me for allowing my love to grow cold and for getting caught up in routine. Renew my passion and devotion, and draw me closer to You each Day. May my service be an expression of my love for You, filled with joy and gratitude. Amen.

PERSONAL REFLECTION:

How can I rekindle my love for Christ and prioritize my relationship with Him? What steps can I take to return to the joy and passion of my first love.

DAY 86: THE CHURCH OF SMYRNA – FAITHFUL UNTO DEATH

Scripture: Revelation 2:10 (NASB)
"Do not fear what you are about to suffer. Behold, the devil is about to cast some of you into prison, so that you will be tested, and you will have tribulation for ten days. Be faithful until death, and I will give you the crown of life."

ANECDOTE:

A soldier is given a challenging mission, knowing that it will be dangerous and that he may face great suffering. Despite the risks, he remains committed to his duty, motivated by his love for his country and his fellow soldiers. His courage and faithfulness inspire those around him, even in the face of adversity.

APPLICATION:

The church in Smyrna faced persecution, suffering, and trials. Jesus encouraged them not to fear but to remain faithful, promising them the crown of life. This message reminds us that suffering and trials are a part of the Christian life, but they are temporary compared to the eternal reward that awaits us. Faithfulness in the midst of suffering is a testimony of our trust in God and His promises.

Being faithful unto death means holding on to our faith, even when it costs us. It means trusting God's sovereignty, knowing that He is with us in every trial. Jesus Himself endured suffering and death, and He calls us to follow His example. The crown of life is a reward for those who persevere, reflecting God's approval and love. Let us remain faithful, knowing that our suffering is not in vain and that God's promise of eternal life is sure.

FURTHER SCRIPTURE:

- James 1:12: Blessed is the man who perseveres under trial, for he will receive the crown of life.
- 2 Timothy 4:7-8: Paul speaks of fighting the good fight, finishing the race, and receiving the crown of righteousness.
- Romans 8:18: The sufferings of this present time are not worth comparing with the glory that will be revealed in us.

PRAYER:

Heavenly Father, give me the strength to remain faithful in the face of trials and suffering. Help me not to fear but to trust in Your promises and Your presence. May my faithfulness be a testimony of my love for You, and may I hold on to the hope of the crown of life. Thank You for Your faithfulness and the assurance of eternal life. Amen.

PERSONAL REFLECTION:

How can I remain faithful in the midst of trials and suffering? What steps can I take to strengthen my trust in God's promises and His presence?

DAY 87: THE CHURCH OF PERGAMUM – HOLDING FAST TO THE TRUTH

Scripture: Revelation 2:13 (NASB)
*"I know where you dwell, where Satan's throne is; and
you hold fast My name, and did not deny My faith
even in the days of Antipas, My faithful witness, who
was killed among you, where Satan dwells."*

ANECDOTE:

A lighthouse stands on a rocky shore, its light shining brightly in the darkness. Despite the strong winds and crashing waves, the lighthouse remains steadfast, guiding ships safely to shore. The light does not waver, offering hope and direction to those navigating through the storm.

APPLICATION:

The church in Pergamum lived in a challenging environment, surrounded by idolatry and false teachings. Despite this, they held fast to the name of Jesus and did not deny their faith. Jesus commended them for their steadfastness but also warned them against tolerating false teachings. This message reminds us of the importance of holding fast to the truth of God's Word, even in the face of opposition or pressure to compromise.

Holding fast to the truth means knowing God's Word, standing firm in our beliefs, and rejecting anything that contradicts the gospel. It involves being vigilant against false teachings and influences that can lead us astray. In a world where truth is often distorted, we are called to be like a lighthouse, shining the light of God's truth and offering hope to others. Let us hold fast to the truth, knowing that Jesus is our anchor and His Word is our guide.

FURTHER SCRIPTURE:

- 2 Timothy 3:16-17: All Scripture is God-breathed and useful for teaching, rebuking, correcting, and training in righteousness.
- Ephesians 4:14-15: Speak the truth in love, growing in every way more like Christ.
- Psalm 119:105: Your word is a lamp to my feet and a light to my path.

PRAYER:

Lord, help me to hold fast to Your truth, even when faced with opposition or temptation to compromise. Give me discernment to recognize false teachings and the courage to stand firm in my faith. May my life reflect the light of Your truth, guiding others to know You. Thank You for Your Word, which is a lamp to my feet and a light to my path. Amen.

PERSONAL REFLECTION:

How can I hold fast to the truth of God's Word in my daily life? What steps can I take to guard against false teachings and influences that may lead me astray?

DAY 88: THE CHURCH OF THYATIRA – GROWING IN LOVE AND SERVICE

Scripture: Revelation 2:19 (NASB)
"I know your deeds, and your love and faith and service and perseverance, and that your deeds of late are greater than at first."

ANECDOTE:

A gardener tends to a young plant, watering it and providing the necessary care. Over time, the plant grows, producing beautiful flowers and bearing fruit. The gardener's attention and care have paid off, resulting in a thriving, vibrant garden. The growth is evident and brings joy to all who see it.

APPLICATION:

The church in Thyatira was commended for their love, faith, service, and perseverance. Jesus noted that their deeds were greater than they were at first, indicating spiritual growth and maturity. This message encourages us to continue growing in our love for God and others, serving faithfully, and persevering in our faith. Spiritual growth is a continuous process that involves nurturing our relationship with God, serving others, and remaining steadfast in our commitment to Christ.

Growing in love and service means putting our faith into action, showing kindness and compassion to those around us. It involves being patient, forgiving, and willing to serve, even when it's challenging. Perseverance is key, as it keeps us moving forward, trusting in God's strength and grace. Let us strive to grow in love and service, knowing that our deeds bring glory to God and reflect His love to the world.

FURTHER SCRIPTURE:

- Galatians 5:6: The only thing that counts is faith expressing itself through love.
- 1 Corinthians 15:58: Be steadfast, immovable, always abounding in the work of the Lord.
- Hebrews 6:10: God is not unjust; He will not forget your work and the love you have shown Him as you have helped His people.

PRAYER:

Lord, thank You for the example of the church in Thyatira, who grew in love, faith, service, and perseverance. Help me to follow their example, growing in my love for You and others, serving faithfully, and persevering in my faith. May my deeds bring glory to Your name and reflect Your love to those around me. Strengthen me to continue growing in my walk with You. Amen.

PERSONAL REFLECTION:

In what ways can I grow in love, service, and perseverance? How can I put my faith into action and serve others with a heart of love and compassion?

DAY 89: THE CHURCH OF SARDIS – WAKE UP AND STRENGTHEN WHAT REMAINS

Scripture: Revelation 3:2 (NASB)
"Wake up, and strengthen the things that remain, which were about to die; for I have not found your deeds completed in the sight of My God."

ANECDOTE:

A student falls asleep while studying for an important exam. When he wakes up, he realizes that time has slipped away, and he hasn't completed his preparations. With renewed urgency, he focuses on his studies, knowing that there is still time to prepare and succeed. His awareness of the urgency motivates him to stay awake and give his best effort.

APPLICATION:

The church in Sardis had a reputation for being alive, but Jesus saw that they were spiritually asleep and needed to wake up. His message was a call to revival, to strengthen what remained, and to complete the work God had given them. This message reminds us of the importance of spiritual vigilance and the need to stay awake and alert in our faith.

Waking up spiritually means examining our hearts, repenting of complacency, and renewing our commitment to Christ. It involves seeking God's guidance, staying connected to His Word, and being active in our faith. Strengthening what remains means nurturing our relationship with God, growing in our knowledge of Him, and using our gifts to serve others. Let us heed the call to wake up and strengthen our faith, knowing that God has a purpose for our lives and work for us to do.

FURTHER SCRIPTURE:

- Romans 13:11: The hour has come for you to wake up from your slumber, because our salvation is nearer now than when we first believed.
- Ephesians 5:14: Wake up, sleeper, rise from the dead, and Christ will shine on you.
- 1 Thessalonians 5:6: Let us not sleep as others do, but let us be alert and sober.

PRAYER:

Lord, help me to wake up spiritually and to be vigilant in my faith. Forgive me for any complacency or neglect in my walk with You. Strengthen what remains in my heart, and guide me to complete the work You have given me. May my life be a reflection of Your light, and may I remain faithful to Your calling. Amen.

PERSONAL REFLECTION:

How can I wake up spiritually and strengthen my relationship with God? What steps can I take to remain vigilant and active in my faith?

DAY 90: THE CHURCH OF PHILADELPHIA – AN OPEN DOOR

Scripture: Revelation 3:8 (NASB)
"I know your deeds. Behold, I have put before you an open door which no one can shut, because you have a little power, and have kept My word, and have not denied My name."

ANECDOTE:

A young artist receives an unexpected opportunity to showcase her work in a prominent gallery. The open door leads to new connections, growth, and the chance to share her talent with a wider audience. She recognizes that this opportunity is a gift, and she steps through the door with confidence, knowing that it could change her future.

APPLICATION:

The church in Philadelphia was commended for their faithfulness, and Jesus set before them an open door that no one could shut. This open door represents opportunities for ministry, growth, and sharing the gospel. Jesus' message to the church in Philadelphia reminds us that when we remain faithful, God opens doors for us that no one can close.

Being faithful with the opportunities God gives us means stepping through the open doors with trust and obedience. It involves being bold in sharing our faith, serving others, and using our gifts for God's glory. Even when we feel we have little power, God's strength is made perfect in our weakness. Let us walk through the open doors God places before us, trusting that He is with us and that He has a purpose for our lives.

FURTHER SCRIPTURE:

- Colossians 4:3: Pray for us that God may open a door for our message, so that we may proclaim the mystery of Christ.
- 1 Corinthians 16:9: A great door for effective work has opened to me, and there are many adversaries.
- 2 Corinthians 2:12: The Lord opened a door for me to preach the gospel.

PRAYER:

Lord, thank You for the open doors You place before me. Help me to recognize and walk through these opportunities with faith and obedience. Strengthen me to share the gospel, serve others, and use my gifts for Your glory. May my life be a reflection of Your love and truth, and may I trust in Your guidance and provision. Amen.

PERSONAL REFLECTION:

What open doors has God placed before me, and how can I be faithful in stepping through them? How can I use my gifts and opportunities to serve God and share the gospel with others?

DAY 91: THE CHURCH OF LAODICEA – LUKEWARM NO MORE

Scripture: Revelation 3:15-16 (NASB)
"I know your deeds, that you are neither cold nor hot; I wish that you were cold or hot. So because you are lukewarm, and neither hot nor cold, I will spit you out of My mouth."

ANECDOTE:

A coffee shop serves both hot and iced coffee, catering to customers' preferences. However, a cup of lukewarm coffee left sitting on the counter goes untouched. It lacks the refreshing coolness of iced coffee or the comforting warmth of a hot brew. Lukewarm coffee fails to satisfy, and most people prefer to avoid it.

APPLICATION:

The church in Laodicea was neither hot nor cold but lukewarm, and Jesus warned them of the consequences. This message serves as a powerful reminder that complacency and indifference in our faith are dangerous. Jesus desires that we be passionate and committed in our relationship with Him, not lukewarm or half-hearted.

Being lukewarm means going through the motions without true devotion, allowing the cares of this world to dull our spiritual fervor. Jesus calls us to repent and renew our passion for Him. He stands at the door and knocks, inviting us into a deeper, more vibrant relationship with Him. Let us be zealous, seeking God with all our heart, and living out our faith with enthusiasm and commitment. Lukewarm no more, we are called to be on fire for God, making a difference in the world for His kingdom.

FURTHER SCRIPTURE:

- Romans 12:11: Never be lacking in zeal, but keep your spiritual fervor, serving the Lord.
- Matthew 5:16: Let your light shine before others, that they may see your good deeds and glorify your Father in heaven.
- Jeremiah 29:13: You will seek Me and find Me when you seek Me with all your heart.

PRAYER:

Lord Jesus, forgive me for any lukewarmness in my faith. Help me to be passionate and committed in my relationship with You. Renew my zeal and fill me with the fire of Your Spirit. May my life be a reflection of Your love, and may I serve You with enthusiasm and dedication. Teach me to seek You with all my heart and to live out my faith boldly. Amen.

PERSONAL REFLECTION:

In what areas of my life have I become lukewarm? How can I renew my passion for God and live with greater commitment and zeal for His kingdom?

FIRMING UP YOUR FAITH
SEVEN CHURCHES OF REVELATION

- Reflect on the message to the church at Ephesus. What steps can you take to remember your first love?

- How does the example of faithfulness from the church at Smyrna encourage you?

- In what ways can you hold fast to the truth, as the church at Pergamum was encouraged to do?

- How does the call to grow in love and service resonate with you, as seen in the church at Thyatira?

- What actions can you take to strengthen your spiritual life, as urged for the church at Sardis?

- How does the open door given to the church at Philadelphia inspire your faith?

- Reflect on the church at Laodicea's message. What can you do to be more fervent in your walk with Christ?

DEAR READER,

Thank you for joining me on this journey through *Foundations of Faith*. My prayer is that each day's devotional has encouraged you, challenged you, and helped deepen your trust and faith in our Lord Jesus Christ. As you continue to walk with Him, may you experience the fullness of His love, the strength of His presence, and the peace that surpasses all understanding.

Remember, your faith is a foundation upon which God will continue to build. Trust Him in all things, seek His guidance daily, and know that He is faithful to complete the work He has begun in you. As you go forward, I want you to know that I will be praying for you. I pray that God will strengthen your faith, guide your steps, and fill your heart with His love and joy. May you continue to grow in the knowledge of His grace and be a light to others, sharing the hope that is found in Christ alone.

Please, drop me a note at info@jehovahjirehministries.com and let me know what you think about this devotional.

Thank you for allowing me to be a part of your spiritual journey. I look forward to what God has in store for you.

In Christ's love,
Dr. Ralph W. Jenkins

COMING SOON

TITLE: THE ROMANS ROAD
SUBTITLE: A JOURNEY THROUGH THE BOOK OF ROMANS, A DAY BY DAY DEVOTIONAL

Explore the profound truths of the book of Romans in this daily devotional, designed to take you on a journey through one of the most theologically rich books of the Bible. Whether you are a new believer or have been walking with Christ for years, *The Romans Road* will encourage and challenge you, deepening your understanding of the doctrines of faith and the incredible grace of God.

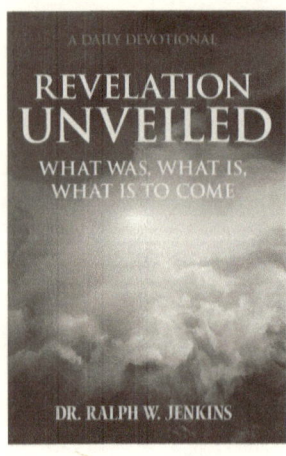

TITLE: REVELATION UNVEILED
SUBTITLE: WHAT WAS, WHAT IS, WHAT IS TO COME, A DAY BY DAY DEVOTIONAL

Delve into the mysteries of the book of Revelation with *Revelation Unveiled*. This devotional will guide you through the past, present, and future as revealed by the Apostle John, offering insights into God's plan for humanity and His eternal kingdom. Designed to both encourage and challenge, this devotional will help you understand the powerful messages contained in Revelation and apply them to your daily life.

www.ingramcontent.com/pod-product-compliance
Lightning Source LLC
Chambersburg PA
CBHW020230130626
46549CB00005B/1827